Loyalty to the Kingdom of Christ

Loyalty to the Kingdom of Christ

Christian Responsibility in Politics and Society

Sven Pearl Johanson

The Hermit Kingdom Press
Cheltenham • Seoul • Bangalore • Cebu

LOYALTY TO THE KINGDOM OF CHRIST: CHRISTIAN RESPONSIBILITY IN POLITICS AND SOCIETY

Copyright © 2004 by Sven Pearl Johanson

All rights reserved. No part of this book may be produced in any form or by any means, electronic or mechanical, including photocopying, recording, or by any information storage retrieval system, without permission in writing from the publisher.

ISBN: 0-9723864-9-1

Write To Address:
The Hermit Kingdom Press
3741 Walnut Street, Suite 407
Philadelphia, PA 19104
United States of America
http://www.TheHermitKingdomPress.com

Library of Congress Control Number: 2004112460

Dedicated to Christians
of every nationality, race, and background
who strive to remain faithful
to Jesus Christ,
the King of kings
and the LORD of lords
even to the point of death

CONTENTS

Introduction <11>

Chapter 1: Jesus Christ as the King of Kings <21>

Chapter 2: Christians as Citizens of the Kingdom of Christ <47>

Chapter 3: Christian Loyalty and Political Obligation <61>

Chapter 4: Christian Loyalty and Social Obligation <105>

Chapter 5: Christian Loyalty and Christian Holy War <147>

Conclusion <169>

"As a utopian group, the counterculture understands something very real, both as to the culture as a culture, but also as to the poverty of modern man's concept of nature and the way the machine is eating up nature on every side."

Francis A. Schaeffer

Introduction

What does loyalty to Jesus Christ, the King of kings, entail? This is a question that not many Christians today ask actively or openly. But this is a question that is becoming increasingly important in today's political setting.

Consider this scenario. If the United Kingdom, under Tony Blair, passes laws targeting so-called religious intolerance, a Baptist preacher who preaches that Jesus Christ is the King of kings can possibly be arrested. The law which Tony Blair and the British Labour Party want to pass makes it illegal to make exclusive claims. So, a Charismatic preacher proclaiming that the only way to salvation is through the Lord Jesus Christ would be committing an illegal act. Under the new British law (if passed), the Charismatic minister of Christ can be arrested and put in jail with mass murderers.

The new law (if passed) of the United Kingdom will consider a Catholic priest a criminal if he preaches that those who do not believe in Jesus Christ as God will go to Hell. Why? The Labour Party of the United Kingdom would consider this a type of religious incitement to potential violence.

Under this law which the British Labour Party has been trying to pass for years and will continue to do so if they are elected again to power

Introduction

(certainly under Tony Blair's leadership), reading the Gospel accounts literally of how Jews cried, "Crucify Him! Crucify Him!" would constitute a criminal offense. Any Baptist pastor preaching literally from the Passion Narratives of Jesus Christ can be arrested and put in prison with terrorists.

British Christians are living under a real threat against Christianity. Some people point to secular Jews with an agenda against Christianity as the culprits in Britain. It is no secret that British politics has powerful Jews playing very important roles. Britain is the only country in the West to have had a Jewish Prime Minister (equivalent to the US President).

It was the United Kingdom that gave its colony of Palestine to a bunch of white European Jews. British nobility who are Jews played a crucial role in the handing over the British colony of Palestine to white European Jews to found the Zionist project. The rhetoric that Zionist Jews used was distinctively anti-Christian as many published books and writings by Zionists attest. So, it is more than plausible that modern British Jews in power positions are carrying on the anti-Christian sentiments of key Zionist leaders and trying to target Christianity through these religious laws. These Jews would like nothing more than to change the Gospel accounts to make Jews (Pharisees and Sadducees) heroes and Jesus into an evil figure.

Whatever the motivations behind the new laws that Tony Blair and the Labour Party are trying to pass, the anti-Christian character is clear. An anti-Christian stance of British Jews who play powerful political roles should come as no surprise to Americans. We know what secular Jews are capable of. Jewish organizations have sued working-class Irish Catholic towns to get rid of Nativity scenes in front of town halls during Christmas time. Many working class Irish Catholic families in New England are personally witnesses to the struggle against anti-Catholic sentiments of Jews. Many working-class Irish Catholic children in New England remember Ivy League educated Jewish lawyers coming into their working class town and stripping it of one public, shared positive experience; namely, the Nativity Scene at Christmas time. Now grown, these Irish Catholic individuals remember with bitterness how Jews came in and humiliated their parents and their town leaders, while draining their working class town of communal funds through law suits after law suits.

Americans also know that Jews have been very active in the Democratic Party. Some of the top leaders in the Democratic Party have exhibited anti-Christian sentiments and tried to push anti-Christian policies. Not surprisingly, many of them are descendants of anti-Christian Zionists. It is no secret that many Christian organizations perceive anti-Christian Jewish groups and individuals as a threat to Christianity and individual Christians in America. And Americans sometimes wonder what would happen if these anti-Christian Jews will rise to power and legislate against Christianity.

Christians have been persecuted by Jews before, so it will be nothing new. The Book of Acts describes Pharisees as going from city to city to hunt down Jews who have converted to Christianity and no longer held to an identity within Judaism. St. Stephen was killed by the Jewish masses at the instigation of Jewish religious and political leaders. If Jews in Britain or in the USA legislated against Christians and started persecuting Christians, it would be like the first century AD at the time of Jesus Christ and St. Paul. It happened then, and it could happen now.

As an organized group, Jews are the most likely to advance anti-Christian legislation than anyone else. Muslims do not have power in the West. No Muslim group is organized to the extent that it can overturn laws in the West. Jewish groups are.

Furthermore, Muslims do not have a history of persecuting Christians in the style of Jews. Islam lacks a large body of anti-Christian writings as it is the case in Judaism. Since the birth of Jesus Christ, Jews have attacked Christianity vigorously. There are printed and published (many actually pro-actively supported by Jewish communities) writings against Christianity in the last 2,000 years. Anti-Christianity is internalized in Jewish communities the way it is not in any other religious communities, including Muslim.

So, if any group will have a bearing on passing anti-Christian laws, it will be from the Jews. Jews, particularly secular Jews, move freely in Western societies and educational circles. Secular Jews, often being white and indistinguishable visually from white Gentiles, can easily blend in and progress through the social and corporate ranks, which often bar the people of color. It is simply a fact that many Jews in Britain and in the USA are in power positions to impact legislation and public discourse. It is also a fact that many Jews in prominent positions in the United Kingdom and the USA (and elsewhere in Europe, Australia, and New Zealand) owe greater allegiance to Jews and distrust Gentiles. This is true even for many secular Jews.

Perhaps, Zionism impacted all Jews in a way to homogenize a sentiment of distrust of Gentiles.

The fact is that because these Jews run in social circles and are prominent as academics, businesspersons, and policy makers, many Christians are in a state of a bind. These Jews in prominent positions can be our bosses who have the power to promote us or demote us in the workplace. Even if they used their Jewish loyalties to punish us, there is little recourse for Christians. And most Christians working under Jewish bosses have a family to think about. No Christian father or mother would want to jeopardize their children's future or livelihood unnecessarily. When Jewish bosses use their Jewish interests to manipulate, it is difficult for Christian workers to stand up for the Christian faith or for Jesus Christ, the King of kings. A Christian's loyalty is tested in the work place. It is difficult to be loyal to Jesus Christ when you don't see Him. You do see your Jewish boss and your paycheck.

Similar kind of social situation exists at the highest levels of government. There will be Jewish bosses who will want to advance Jewish interests and browbeat Christians (pushing the limits but still being in the gray zone). A Christian in government and government positions may have to choose between being loyal to Jesus Christ, the King of kings, and possibly being demoted or even fired, and humoring an anti-Christian Jew and currying favors. Playing Judas Iscariot is quite easy when you can't see Jesus Christ but you see your Jewish boss every day. She can wear your defenses down.

Even if you don't have a Jewish boss, you may have Jewish colleagues and "friends." These Jewish co-workers can wear your Christian defenses down individually. Jewish co-workers can also organize and pressure you as a type of an organized group. This can happen just as easily in a university department as in the US Senate cambers. We are at a time when Christian loyalty to Jesus Christ, the King of kings, is tested in our daily lives. Jewish colleagues and bosses are at the forefront of today's shared experiences for many Christians, particularly in prominent positions.

It is true that Christians often face the problem of suffering professionally at the hands of Jews if we remain faithful to Jesus Christ, the King of kings. Unlike Britain, America may not have to fear going to jail for proclaiming that Jesus Christ is the only savior of the world. However, perhaps through Jewish rise to power or through a combination of factors, a reality exists whereby Christians may be forced to reassess the question of being loyal to Jesus Christ, the King of kings, and facing suffering, jail time, or even death.

This book, therefore, addresses the issue: What does loyalty to Jesus Christ, the King of kings, entail? In answering this question, I will discuss the following topics: (1) Jesus Christ as the King of kings; (2) Christians as citizens of the Kingdom of Christ; (3) Christian loyalty and political obligation; (4) Christian loyalty and social obligations; and (5) Christian loyalty and Christian Holy War.

Chapter 1:

Jesus Christ as the King of Kings

When we Christians think about Jesus Christ, many of His attributes come to mind. All Christians – Catholic, Protestant, Orthodox, and Coptic – are agreed that Jesus is God. The divinity of Jesus Christ is an essential part of the Christian understanding of who Jesus is and what He did/does. Often, we Christians like to talk about Jesus as God Incarnate. Jesus as God came in the human flesh in order to save those who accept Jesus Christ as LORD and Savior. It was Jesus' intention to die on the cross in order to save us in a substitutionary sacrifice needed to take away our sins (liability to punishment) before God. It was God's love that He Himself came down in flesh to save us. The resurrection of Jesus Christ from the dead was a proof-positive that Jesus had conquered sin and that He had secured salvation for all those who would, out of their free-will, choose Jesus Christ as their personal LORD and Savior.

Certainly, Christ's character as God who came in the flesh to save us from our sins is important. Christians throughout 2,000 years of Christian history have affirmed that Jesus is God (Yahweh of the Old Testament). In fact, Christians have argued that Jews rejected Yahweh by rejecting Jesus Christ because Jesus Christ is the God of the

Old Testament, the New Testament, and the present age. Thus, Christians have affirmed that Christians are the true inheritors of the blessings of the Old Testament promised to God's people. Jews have rejected Yahweh by rejecting Jesus Christ, who is Yahweh Himself. Thus, Jews (who are not converted to Christianity) are under the curse of the Old Testament, which was prophesied against Jews who reject Yahweh. Certainly, the Christian understanding of Jesus as God is crucial to understanding Christian self-understanding for the past 2,000 years.

Of course, implicit in the understanding that Jesus is God (Yahweh) is the understanding that Jesus is the King of kings and the LORD or lords. God is described as King of kings and the LORD of lords in the Bible. Certainly, in the Old Testament the royal character of God is affirmed. God is described as the LORD of hosts. In the Hebrew original, "hosts" refer to armies. Thus, God is the God of armies, or a King who leads the holy armies. When we say that Jesus is God (Yahweh), we understand that Jesus owns the divine title of the Old Testament. Jesus Christ is, in fact, the LORD of hosts. Jesus Christ commands holy armies of heaven.

For those who are familiar with the New Testament, it comes as no surprise that Jesus is the LORD of hosts. Jesus Himself describes himself in such terms, particularly in the Son of Man sayings. Jesus often described himself in the Gospels as the apocalyptic judge who will come back in the Last Days in glory. Jesus describes Himself as having the ultimate, royal power to judge the final destiny of every single person in the world. In the Son of Man sayings, it is assumed that Jesus will rightly judge for Jesus is the King of kings and the LORD of lords.

Jesus Christ as the King of kings and the LORD of lords coming back to earth in full glory and with a host of heavenly armies is reiterated throughout the New Testament. The Revelation does not describe Jesus, who humbled Himself to bring us His salvation through the substitutionary death on the cross, but rather Jesus who has no reason to humble Himself to anything. The work of salvation is done and Jesus is the King of kings and the LORD of lords, before whom all in Creation must be humbled.

The New Testament passages describing Jesus' Second Coming, therefore, refuses to portray Jesus as a meek, weak individual, who turns the other cheek when His enemies assail. The Jesus Christ of the Second Coming returns as the King of kings and the LORD of lords, who dictates His own laws and applies it blanketly over the whole world. Jesus Christ of the Second Coming cares less what human laws are, what human ethics demands, and what human sensibilities request. Jesus Christ of the Revelation is an unsympathetic, all powerful King of kings who will instate His rule and judgment, no matter how unjust it may seem to humans.

Jesus Christ of the Apocalypse comes down to install His rule. Those who are followers of Christ will be gathered to Him to rule with Him; those who do not follow Christ are cast aside and thrown into Hell, a place of eternal damnation and eternal suffering. The New Testament assumes that this act of Christ is fundamentally righteous. Christ has the right to send to the eternal holocaust those who reject the rule of Christ as the King of kings and the LORD of lords.

The New Testament assumes that Jesus Christ is the King of kings with absolute power. There is, therefore, no unethical policy for the King of kings. The King of kings can send millions to the eternal holocaust, and He is still righteous. Sending millions to the eternal holocaust is, in fact, a righteous act of Jesus Christ. No one can stand up and oppose Jesus because Jesus is not a democratically elected ruler, a type of primus inter pares. Jesus is God, and we are humans. Jesus can do what He sees fit, and we have no right to protest.

In fact, when Jesus Christ sends millions to the eternal holocaust, Christians will cheer. Christians will celebrate at the Day of Judgment as Jesus Christ condemns millions to the eternal gas chamber of unquenching fire because Christ as the King of kings has chosen to do this. And the New Testament clearly supports this action of Christ as all other actions of Christ. Christ is the King of kings and the LORD of lords with supreme, unquestioned power.

Implicit in this understanding is the acknowledgment that Jesus is God. Jesus is the King of kings and the LORD of lords because He is God (Yahweh). Just as the Old Testament describes God as fundamentally righteous in committing genocide against the people in Sodom and Gomorrah through raining fire down from Heaven, Jesus Christ is portrayed in the New Testament as fundamentally right by sending millions to the eternal gas chamber for eternal suffering and pain.

The New Testament fundamentally supports the idea that God can do anything He pleases. It doesn't matter if it violates human laws, goes against human ethics, or ruffles our human sentiments. Jesus as God is the Creator who has the right to do with His Creation as He pleases. Does the clay have the right to tell the Potter what he should make? The potter can use the clay to make some things for noble purposes and others to be used as refuse. Jesus as God has absolute power to do as He wills. This is the fundamental principle associated with the title of Jesus as the King of kings and the LORD of lords.

Biblical principles outlining the Divine Kingship of Christ is clear. However, it is difficult for humans to grasp what Divine kingship means. That is the reason why the Bible explains Christ's kingship in human terms as well. This helps humans to make a mental transition from the concept of human kingship to the concept of Divine kingship. The chief model to explicate Jesus in terms of human kingship is through the person of King David.

King David has the status of a mythic hero in the Bible. As a young lad, he killed Goliath, the chief enemy of Israelites, single-handedly. Grown men, powerful warriors, time-tested battle commanders, and the Israelite King Saul were no match for Goliath. Goliath is akin to Achilles in his stature as a warrior.

The Bible describes Israelites as being on the verge of defeat in a major war. All in Israel were trembling in fear. David, who was only a young lad, came to Israel's help. No one expected a little boy to deliver them. No one thought there existed anyone who would vanquish the powerful commander of the enemy side. The commander had power, wealth, means, and armies behind him. David was a shepherd boy more accustomed to composing poems than being engaged in a fight.

But there David was, a shepherd poet, who with one stroke vanquished the powerful enemy.

Even after David saved the Israelites, the Israelites did not thank him. Well, they might have said, "Thank you." But soon afterwards, we see David running. David is running and running away from the Israelite army that he just saved. The Israelite army that would have been slaughtered by the mighty commander Goliath and his battle-tested soldiers were now hunting David down. Instead of showing David allegiance for all that he has done for them, they were now out to kill him. The irony might be amusing if it were not so pathetic. King Saul was hunting David down with his Israelite soldiers.

David ran away and perhaps saw Israelite soldiers pointed to that as a sign of weakness. No doubt Saul used the fact that David ran as a sign of his guilt. David was guilty. David had done something wrong. That was why David was running. Saul was right to hunt David down. Israelite soldiers were right to hunt David down. Saul probably tried to convince Israelite soldiers that it was the will of God that they hunt David down.

Saul probably generated a rumor mill. David was impious because he was running. He was not offering sacrifices to God in God's temple. Did the Israelite soldiers see David when the worship of God was in progress? No! Did David read the Bible in the assembly of Bible-reading? Did anyone see David pray? Saul instigated Israelites against David. Saul had a legitimate post. Saul had access to power. Saul hobnobbed with policy makers. Saul was in the power structure. David had nothing. David ran. And in David's absence, King Saul demonized him.

Thus, the hero that saved the Israelites was now hunted down by Israelites. Saul persuaded the Israelite people to reject David. David ran. The pain of David is recounted in his psalms. David had to deal with the rejection of a people he embraced. David had to deal with the fact that the king whom he rescued from Goliath's grips was now out to kill him. Betrayal after betrayal must have worn David down. David cries out in pain in many of his poems. Although David is not portrayed in the Bible as praying like Jacob when his life was endangered, David's poems exhibit an implicit dependence on God. David's biblical poems testify to his reliance on God for salvation. David ran and ran. And David wrote poems as he ran.

God loved David. Thus, God gave David opportunities to kill Saul, more than once. Although David knew he had the opportunity to kill Saul, he chose not to exercise this right. He could have sued for Saul's death, but David was merciful. David gave Saul chances after chances to ask for forgiveness. David gave Saul chances to stop. Saul did not care. Saul wanted to kill David. Like the irrational Pharaoh of the exodus who finally brought down genocide of the firstborn, Saul continued in his evil pursuit of David. Eventually, God compelled the killing of Saul by one whom He designated. Even though David did not kill Saul with his own hands, God raised someone up, when David (or Saul) did not suspect and killed Saul.

After years of being a fugitive, escaping from the law manipulated by evil men, David was installed as king by God. All the laws and soldiers of Israel that persecuted David could not stop God's anointed from having his place in power. Even the soldiers who did evil bidding of those in power eventually gave their allegiance to David to be king over them. Those who tried to kill David at Saul's bidding were now out to kill David's enemies, even risking their own lives.

The age of David the King was the Golden Age for Israel. David the King was triumphant in victories and bravely defended the people under his rule. God blessed David and the wealth of his kingdom increased. A poor shepherd boy running from the law and oppressed by the powerful people, who wrote poems to console himself, now commanded all the wealth and people of the empire. From the depth of utter poverty and helplessness, David rose to the position of supreme power and dominance. This happened in a relatively short time. People who saw David running probably would not have imagined in a million years. It was like the author of Harry Potter books. No one watching her write in a café in Scotland before her fame could have predicted that she would be richer than the Queen of England. This happened in a period of a few years. When God decided to raise David up to power, it was accomplished.

David is portrayed as a righteous king in the Bible. Despite the fact that he committed adultery with Bethsheba and even had her husband killed in a war so that he could keep having sex with her against the 10 commandments, God called David's heart pure. God's concept of a pure heart is not, first and foremost, about sexual purity or not sinning. David is described in the Bible as having a pure heart because despite all his sins, David was loyal to the LORD.

Even when David was running, he trusted the LORD. When David was betrayed by those whom he saved, he still depended on God. Even when David was in a state of utter poverty, he relied on God and thanked Him. Even as he stole food at the Temple and broke the 10 commandment, he implicitly recognized God's greatness.

Jesus, in fact, exonerated David's sin against the 10 commandments when Jesus fought the Pharisees and the Second Temple Jewish laws on purity. For God, purity of heart is not about not committing a sin, but about loyalty to the LORD. Even as David committed adultery and killed innocent people, he had loyalty to the LORD and thus in God's eyes, David's heart was pure.

The Bible is clear in emphasizing that humans sin and that they will always sin until they die. Trying not to sin is encouraged and repentance for sins demanded, but Bible never states that humans can be sinless. To be human is to sin. Only God is sinless. God's standards are different from human standards. Thus, David the adulterer and the murderer of the innocent was a man after God's own heart.

David was certainly loyal to the LORD. David fought those who blasphemed the identity of God with a zeal that is unmatched in the Bible. David sought to annihilate people who tried to defame God by bringing Him down to the human level. And God loved his passionate hatred of those who wanted the LORD to sit at human feet. To murder was righteous and David was eager and passionate about murdering God's enemies. The LORD of Hosts was able to count on David to kill for Him.

Besides killing in allegiance to God, David showed his loyalty to God by emphasizing proper worship of God. The important fact to emphasize is that David upheld the principle of proper worship.

It is important to remember that people are sinners. All people are sinners. Thus, we may not in practice offer proper cultic worship. But that's not what determines the purity of heart. The purity of heart is in the emphasizing of the principles even when those principles will be violated by human weakness the very next day. Even while violating God's principles, those who are pure in heart will uphold God's principles. This is what is meant by pure in heart. What determines the purity of heart is the zeal in upholding principles while recognizing that human weakness will most likely violate it.

This is, of course, in line with the history of Christianity, guided by the power of the Holy Spirit. Christians have upheld the Bible principle that there is always forgiveness in the cross. You can kill 6 million people for 3 years. But in one minute of prayer, if you ask God to forgive you, God will forgive you. Why? God forgives not on account of your goodness but on the goodness of Jesus Christ. Jesus Christ died on the cross to forgive sinners. It doesn't matter if your sin is a white lie or killing of 6 million people. Sin is sin. God will forgive if you ask God for forgiveness.

So, if Hitler asked God to forgive him and uttered a prayer to accept Jesus Christ as his LORD God and savior the minute before he died, he is in heaven now with God rejoicing in his salvation through the death of Jesus Christ on the cross. Jesus Christ's death is that valuable. It is worth more than anything in the world. It is not useless. It is not ineffective. Christ's death on the cross is powerful to forgive all who choose out of their own free will to repent and accept Christ as God. It is the Christian duty to uphold the value of Jesus' death. It is the sign of Christian loyalty to Christ and the recognition of Christ's substitutionary sacrifice on the cross.

David showed this kind of loyalty to God in upholding the principle that the God of the Bible is the true God who should be worshipped. David wanted to build a beautiful house of prayer for God because he loved God and wanted to encourage worship of God. This kind of zeal and loyalty often encourages people in poor countries to gather money to build a beautiful church to worship Christ. Of course, Christ is God and does not need a house to dwell in. But Christians want to have a beautiful church with a cross as a symbol of Christ's presence to honor Him. It is built as a token of love and devotion. Beautiful church is built to encourage worship of Christ. And that's what David wanted. David wanted to build a house of God to encourage worship of God.

King David has a mythic status in the Bible because of his courageous military victories for God and his loyalty to God. King David thus came to symbolize the idea of the anointed one of God. We have to remember that kings were anointed in the Bible. (Christian kings after the time of Jesus were anointed by the Church. This is in explicit recognition that their rule is under that of Christ, the King of kings. In a similar way, US President is sworn in with the Bible. Only kings who will rule their entire lives are anointed, however. Being anointed is not done for a limited-time offices).

And it is this King David who serves as a human model for the Divine Messiah, the Anointed One. And when we look at the account of Jesus, we notice some remarkable similarities. In fact, King David serves as a narrative typology for Jesus

Christ (of course, except for sin, since Christ as God is sinless!).

Jesus, who is God (Yahweh), became Incarnate in order to save all humans who would repent of their own free will (God acknowledges the importance of human free will). But even at his birth, he faced danger. Jesus came to save, but the Jewish King Herod wanted to kill Jesus because he saw Jesus as a threat. King Herod feared that his power would be taken away by Jesus. King Herod was afraid that Jesus would steal his spotlight. King Herod was afraid that Jesus would steal Jewish allegiance away from him, the Jewish king. King Herod, as Jewish king, should have bowed down and worshipped the King of kings, but instead he pursued Jesus Christ to kill Him.

In the fact that a Jewish king tried to kill the life of the Anointed, Jesus shows that David's life was a type of Christ. We can even say that David's life was a picture of what Jesus' life was going to be like. In other words, David's account in the Old Testament was a type of prophecy of Jesus' life. The prophetic picture in the Old Testament found a prophetic fulfillment in the New Testament. Jesus Christ is the fullness of the prophetic picture. We can say that the account of David in the Old Testament exists to glorify Jesus Christ in the New Testament. Just like Saul the Jewish king pursued David, Herod the Jewish king pursued Jesus Christ.

Jesus Christ and his parents fled to Egypt in order to save their lives. We see the irony of this event. Why would Jesus flee to Egypt? There are many countries where He could have fled to. The New Testament clearly shows us that the place is important. Jesus' parents were specifically commanded to go to Egypt. They would find salvation in Egypt. Only by going to Egypt, would Jesus be saved from the Jewish king.

We must recognize the significance of the flight to Egypt. Egypt was the mortal enemy of Israel. The foundation stories that Jewish mothers often told their children involved the evil Egyptians hurting Israelites. Jewish mothers were eager to tell the stories of the servitude under the Egyptians. Egyptians were evil. And it was God who saved Israelites out of Egypt. Egypt represented all that was evil. And it was a show of God's love for Israelites that God brought them out of Egypt.

Every Passover, Jewish children could expect to be reminded of the story of the Exodus. Egyptians were evil. Egypt represented a type of Hell on earth. God's love for Israelites was in God taking Israelites out of Egypt and placing them in Israel. Jewish children would bless the name of God for bringing them out of Egypt. Jewish communities would stress going out of Egypt as God saving them. Going out of Egypt, in fact, was seen as a symbol of Jewish salvation.

But Jesus' parents were commanded to go out of Israel and into Egypt. In Jewish eyes this would be like a command to go to Hell. In other terms, it is like telling a child whose father died in Auschwitz to go to Auschwitz. The command to flee to Egypt away from Israel must be seen in this light. For Jews, this was the ultimate insult. And we must recognize that the insult was intentional.

Not only was the order to go to Egypt an insult, it was a symbolic rejection of the Jews. It was the Jewish king who wanted to kill Jesus. Those who brought the good news of Jesus' birth were not Jews. The wise men who followed the star came from the East. They were Gentiles most likely from the present-day Iran or India. But it is clear that the wise men were not Jewish.

It is ironic that God sent the star to the Gentiles. God brought Gentiles to Israel to show the Jewish king that he should pay homage to Jesus, the King of kings. But when the Jewish king was informed of the prophetic message of God (Yahweh) by Gentile wise men, he did not listen. Just as God hardened the heart of Pharaoh, God hardened the heart of the Jewish king. Instead of going and worshipping Jesus Christ, King Herod devised a way to kill Jesus Christ. The Gentiles are portayed as messengers of God and Jews are portrayed as evil.

King Herod rejecting Jesus Christ is a symbol. Just as in the rejection by Pharaoh, all Egyptians were thought to have rejected God (Yahweh), the Jewish king's rejection symbolized the rejection of Jesus by all Jews. Certainly, not all Jews rejected Jesus. Perhaps, the shepherds were Jewish (although it is possible that they were itinerant shepherds, such as the Bedouins, and of the Arab race). But it was likely that not all Egyptians took the same position as the Pharaoh. But the Pharaoh as the symbolic representative bore the responsibility of all Egyptians. In the same way, King Herod symbolized the Jewish people in the New Testament. When God killed the first born of Egypt, it included all Egyptians, both those who hated Israelites as well as those who might have been sympathetic to Israelites. When God rejected Pharaoh, God rejected all Egyptians. In the same sense, rejection of the Jewish king symbolizes rejection of all Jews.

Of course, it is important to point out the claims of the Gospels. The Gospel of John teaches us that when we accept Jesus Christ as God, we are born-again. Thus, a Jew can be born a Jew and be under the collective curse as symbolized in the rejection of the Jewish king, those Jews who accept Jesus as God are born again. These Jews become Christians. The old has gone, and, behold, the new has come! Thus, Jews are able to escape condemnation by rejecting Judaism and accepting Jesus Christ as personal Savior and God.

It is important to recognize the rejection of Jews that is emphasized in the New Testament. The command to find salvation in Egypt is only one example of clearly visible proclamation in the New Testament of Jews as a people of God (Yahweh). Jesus was to abandon Jews and go to Jewish enemies. The enemies of Jews will give protection to Jesus and His parents. Jews will give only danger and death. This is what the flight to Egypt showed.

The idea that Jews are a rejected people is clear in other persecutions of Jesus Christ by Jewish leaders. It is not only the Jewish king who sought to kill Jesus. Jewish religious leaders sought to kill Jesus Christ.

The account of the Pharisees and the Sadducees trying to kill Jesus Christ would be pure tragedy if it were not so pathetic. Jesus is described in the Gospel as preaching the Good News. Jesus was doing no one any harm. Jesus was talking. Jesus was talking about how people can be saved. It was clear that Jesus' message that His primary goal was to save.

However, the Pharisees and the Sadducees were a complicated lot. They were convinced that Jesus was against them and that His intentions were evil. Thus, the Pharisees and the Sadducees worked hard to entrap Jesus. These Jewish religious leaders were not interested in hearing Jesus out. The Jewish religious leaders were not interested in reflection or contemplation on what Jesus said. The Jewish leaders were merely interested in entrapping Jesus Christ.

The Jewish leaders rejected Jesus Christ and His message. The Jewish leaders were incapable of seeing Jesus Christ as anything more than their worst enemy. Thus, in the same way Herod sought to kill Jesus, the Jewish religious leaders sought to kill Jesus. The difference was, King Herod had soldiers at his disposal whereas the Jewish religious leaders tried to find a way to bring litigation against Jesus in order to have Him condemned to death. Their evil intention and goals, therefore, can be described as very "Jewish" at the time of Jesus.

Whereas King Herod perceived Jesus as a potential threat to his rule, Jewish religious leaders presumed Jesus to be a threat to Judaism and its survival. Looking at the Gospels, we see that Jewish understanding of Jesus as being anti-Jewish is founded on evidence. It is true that Jesus tried to destroy the essential element of Judaism.

The most prominent rejection of Judaism is seen in Jesus' rejection of Jewish purity laws. The concept of purity was very important to the Jews of Jesus' time. All religious Jews, regardless of which group they belonged to, emphasized ritual purity. It is not like the present-day America, where Reformed Jews have no regard for purity laws. Everything goes for Reformed Jews. It is possible for a Jew to say that they are Reformed Jews even if they do not observe any of the Jewish law books. It was not that way at the time of Jesus. For a Jew to claim that he was religiously Jewish, he had to deserve Jewish purity laws. Even the Dead Sea Scrolls, which describe a small sectarian group, show their commonality with major Jewish religious groups and movements in their emphasis of purity laws.

Jesus, however, rejected Jewish purity laws and brought down the persecution of Jewish religious leaders. Jesus is famous for saying that it is not what goes into a person's mouth that brings impurity but rather what comes out of a person's mouth. The point was that God knows the sinfulness of the human heart. What a person says, such as gossip and slander, portray that person's heart as sinful. Sinfulness is not outside of the person but inside the person.

Obviously, Jesus was targeting Judaism. Judaism focused on purity laws. Jews were allowed to eat only kosher food in keeping with Jewish religious law. Anyone under Judaism eating unkosher food was contaminating himself. Jewish religious leaders emphasized the importance of Jewish purity laws in regards to food. To be a Jew, according to religious Jewish leaders, was to eat kosher food. Consumption of kosher food determined Jewish identity. If a Jew said that he was a Jew but did not consume kosher food, he was not really considered a Jew by religious Jews.

Jewish kosher laws were so important to being Jewish that Jews went to war against a mighty empire to preserve it. When Antiochus IV Epiphanes decreed that no Jews were allowed to eat kosher foods, the Maccabees rose up and fought. Jews rose up with the Maccabees and triumphantly instated their Jewish way of life. American Jews celebrate Hanukkah and this represents the triumph of kosher food laws in the Maccabean battle. Just as Jews in America take pride in celebrating Hanukah, Jews at the time of Jesus took pride in Hanukah, which represented triumph of Jewish food laws through warfare. But unlike America, where many Jews do not observe the spirit of Hanukah, Jews at the time of Jesus celebrated the spirit of the triumph of kosher laws. Thus, for a Jew to be a Jew in the ancient world, she had to observe kosher food laws.

When Jesus preached against kosher food laws, Jesus was preaching against Judaism. In fact, Jesus was attacking the heart of Judaism. It is difficult for Americans to appreciate because the majority of the Jews are not kosher. Majority of American Jews enjoy unkosher food, like bacon and lobster. Many Jewish comedians and actors do not observe kosher laws. And in TV, characters that are portrayed as Jewish are seen as not valuing kosher laws for their Jewish identity. It is easy to let the reality of American Jewish experience to skew the understanding of ancient Judaism. Judaism in Jesus' time was very different from secular Judaism that Reformed Jews in America embrace.

In the ancient world, being a Jew meant keeping the kosher laws. This was particularly important post-Maccabean Revolt. Certainly, during the time of Jesus, this was seen as a fact. A Jew is a Jew when he is kosher.

One can see that the modern State of Israel buys into this value of Jewish identity. It is not surprising given the fact that Zionism tried to combine European nationalism with values of ancient Judaism. The Jewish State was to be a state for Jews that upheld Jewish laws. Since Jewish kosher laws have been a central part of ancient Jewish laws, it naturally became a part of the important values for the Jewish State. Currently, you would be hard-pressed to find any unkosher grocery store in the State of Israel.

Whether you like it or not, all food in an Israeli market is kosher. It is a given in the State of Israel that being Jewish involves keeping kosher. With this belief, the Jewish State, in essence, imposes by law the kosher law on all its citizens, whether secular or religious Jews.

This current reality of the State of Israel helps us to see the condition of ancient Israel. Jews at the time of Jesus assumed that being Jewish was to keep kosher laws. And Jewish religious leaders made sure that food being sold were kosher as much as possible under Roman Empire rule.

For Jesus to tell Jews not to keep kosher was to tell them to stop being Jews. It is not what went inside the mouth that made them impure but what came out of their mouth. Jesus was evangelizing the Jews by attacking what was central to Jewish identity at His time. Jesus was telling Jews to proactively reject their Jewishness. This is understandable since Jesus wanted Jews to reject Judaism. Jesus wanted Jews to accept the fact that Jesus Christ is the Divine Messiah. Jesus wanted the Jews to believe that only He could save them from their sins.

Jesus did not only reject Jewish religious laws in principle. Jesus actively violated Jewish purity laws. Jesus' disciples are encouraged not to wash their hands before meals as demanded by Jewish purity laws. This is understandable because Jesus did not want his disciples to continue being Jewish. Jesus wanted his disciples to abandon Judaism and embrace Christianity. The Pharisees and the Sadducees rightly pick up on Jesus' anti-

Jewish attitude. The Jewish teachers of the Law call Jesus to task for violating Jewish food laws. And Jesus fights with Jewish religious leaders vigorously. Jesus was interested in rejecting Judaism and celebrating Christianity.

It is no surprise that Jewish religious leaders wanted to kill Jesus. Jesus posed a threat to Judaism. They were correct to assume that Jesus despised Judaism. Jesus' disdain for the central purity law of Judaism is a clear evidence of Jesus' hatred of Judaism and what it stood for. Jesus was not polite about his position, either. Jesus insulted Jewish religious leaders to their faces. Christians in America may consider Jesus very brave for doing this, but the Jews at Jesus' time hated Jesus for this.

Jewish religious leaders probably also felt a threat to their personal leadership. Because Jesus answered the Jewish leaders effectively, as described in the New Testament, Jesus made advances in converting Jews to Christianity. Many Jews became followers of Christ. As more and more Jews abandoned Judaism and followed Jesus, Jewish leaders probably felt jealousy and envy. Jewish leaders most likely developed a personal hatred for Jesus. They probably felt that they were losing Jews to Jesus. So, the Jewish religious leaders plotted to kill Jesus Christ.

What the Jewish religious leaders did not understand was that Jesus was claiming Himself as the King of kings and the LORD of lords. Jesus Christ had the right to tell Jews that they must reject kosher food laws to be saved. Jesus had the right as the King of kings to say that the law for God's people that He was instituting was that Jews accept Jesus Christ as their personal Savior and follow

Christian laws. To accept Jewish laws was to reject Jesus Christ, the King of kings.

Thus, the test of faith came to be in the rejection of Jewish purity laws. Did the Jews believe in Jesus Christ as the King of kings and the LORD of lords? If they did, then they had to give up what they deemed most valuable to Judaism. They had to choose between Judaism and Jesus Christ. They had to decide between Jewish purity laws and Jesus Christ. Jesus wanted to see in whom the Jews will put their faith. The result was simple. Jews who refused to reject Judaism and accept Jesus Christ as the King of kings and the LORD of lords would suffer eternal holocaust in Hell. However, those who accepted Jesus Christ as King of kings and the LORD of lords by publicly rejecting Jewish purity laws would have eternal life with Christ and participate in the Kingdom of Christ. The choice was between the Kingdom of Jews and the Kingdom of Christ. Jesus Christ forced Jews to make a decision one way or the other. Jesus Christ took away the gray zone.

The public rejection of Jewish purity laws must be seen in light of Jesus' proclamation to be God (Yahweh). God had the right to establish laws, abolish laws, and fulfill laws. Jesus' divinity is encapsulated in the title of being the King of kings and the LORD or lords. People could understand this concept. Kings had the right to make laws, change laws, and abolish laws. Jesus is the King of kings. This means that Jesus can do what He wills with any human law in existence. In the Bible, Jesus chose to abolish Jewish purity laws. Those who accepted Jesus had to agree with Jesus' position against Jewish purity laws. Being loyal to Jesus Christ meant submitting oneself under the

Law of Christ, the King of kings and the LORD of lords.

It is not surprising that Jesus set out laws for His Kingdom, like any king would. Jesus is the King of kings. The question remains if this Law of Christ is applicable today. I would say that it is. Anyone submitting under the Law of Christ by accepting Jesus Christ as God (Yahweh) must reject Jewish purity laws. This may not be as relevant for Gentiles who do not keep kosher any way. But Jesus' rejection of purity laws is certainly applicable to Jews who accept Jesus Christ. Jews who accept Jesus Christ as the King of kings must cease being kosher personally. Being kosher represents a direct revolt against the Kingdom of Christ. A Christian being kosher in principle (and practice) is an insult to Jesus Christ. Jesus Christ made it clear that He opposes Jewish purity laws. To uphold it would be mutiny in the Kingdom of Christ. To keep kosher in principle is to reject Jesus Christ as the King of kings.

There is a reason why St. Paul takes such an aggressive attitude against Jewish purity laws. Perhaps, Paul, more than any other Christian leader at the time, understood Jewish purity laws and their significance. St. Paul, before he was converted to Christianity, persecuted Jews who converted to Christianity. Paul (as Saul) had the approval and support of Judaism to carry out the persecution of Christians. Before his conversion, Paul was a Pharisee who was zealous about observing Jewish purity laws. He knew the Jewish laws. So, St. Paul spoke from the vantage point of knowledge.

But more importantly, St. Paul understood that Jesus Himself opposed Jewish purity laws. St. Paul understood the implications from the vantage point of the establishment of the Law of Christ. To be Christian required rejection of Judaism and its central public symbols, including the Jewish Law. St. Paul decided to be loyal to Christ, the King of kings, and exhorted Christians towards this loyalty.

It is the central idea of Christianity to recognize that Jesus Christ is the King of kings. Jesus Christ set His kingdom in direct opposition to Judaism. All of the fights that Jesus had with Jewish religious leaders have a point. It is important for Christians around the world to recognize the wishes of the King of kings and the LORD of lords.

It is important because Christians belong to the Kingdom of Christ. Jesus Christ, who is God (Yahweh), took on human flesh to come and save us from our sins. Jesus Christ, the King of kings and the LORD of lords, subjected Himself to a humiliating death on the cross instigated by Jews to bring salvation to those who would choose to believe in Jesus Christ out of their own free will. The salvation that we have in Christ is an infinite debt that cannot be repaid. We are, indeed, saved by grace. But if we belong to the Kingdom of Christ, we now have obligations to this kingdom. Christians must think more seriously about what it means to be citizens of the Kingdom of Christ. And it is to this important responsibility that I will now turn.

Chapter 2:

Christians as Citizens of the Kingdom of Christ

What does it mean for Christians to be citizens in the Kingdom of Christ? This is a very important question for all those who are born again by the mercy and love of Jesus Christ, expressed through His sacrificial death. But all too often, we do not ask this important question. Perhaps, chief among the reasons why we do not ask this question is that the Kingdom of Christ appears to be invisible to us.

Of course, the Kingdom of Christ is very real. And for those who are spiritually in-tune, the Kingdom of Christ is very visible. It is important to emphasize again that Christian spirituality is very different from legalistic spirituality, such as found in Judaism. Christian spirituality is focused and centered on the person and work of Jesus Christ. Faith in Christ is the determinative factor for Christian spirituality. A blind faith in Christ, which is child-like in its trust of Christ, determines one's spirituality in Christianity. Everything else is secondary. The just shall live by faith.

People who are certainly likely to miss the reality of the Kingdom of Christ are legalistic people who, like the Pharisees in the New Testament, emphasize legalism and good works over Jesus Christ. The Pharisees were upright individuals in their society. Even Jesus Christ recognized their faithfulness to the law. But for Jesus Christ, this was irrelevant. When Jewish religious leaders rejected Jesus Christ, all of Jewish legal observance was worthless. Jesus condemned the Pharisees and instead embraced "sinners" in society. For Jesus Christ, all of the legal observance and right behavior were useless without the recognition of Jesus Christ as the King of kings and the LORD of lords. The Pharisees could not see the Kingdom of Christ because they were so engrossed in the Law and proper behavior.

Others who are likely to miss the Kingdom of Christ and fail to recognize its real experience are those who do not have a view to the Day of Judgment. The New Testament emphasizes the coming Son of Man in the Last Days. Jesus Christ as the King of kings will descend to judge all, living and the dead. The dead will be raised so that they might be judged. Jesus Christ will come with the full visibility of His power to end the present age and initiate the future age. This is when those who are born again in Christ will begin their fully-realized eternal life in Heaven. Those who are not born again in Jesus Christ will be cast way into the eternal holocaust in Hell.

Jesus emphasizes that the new age will be different from this age. Family relationships are redefined. All who are born again will be in the family of Christ. Only those who are born again in Christ can belong to this family. So, for instance, if your mother does not believe in Jesus Christ, she will not belong in the family of Christ. If you are born again, you will be in Heaven, but if your mother is not born again, she will be in Hell.

It may seem very sad for someone with a non-Christian mother to contemplate. On earth, we can have emotions for non-Christians. Even when your mother is a non-Christian, you will love her here on earth. This is partly due to the fall of humanity in the Garden of Eden. Before the Fall, all humanity were to live in recognition of Christ as the King of kings and the LORD of lords. But after sin entered the world, humanity has been broken.

Not all human beings recognize Jesus Christ as the King of kings and the LORD of lords. And thus entered the tragedy for humanity. In the same family on earth, it is possible to have those who are Christians and those who are non-Christians. Especially since everyone has the free will to accept Jesus Christ as the Messiah or not, the tragedy is compelled. It's impossible to force someone to convert, to force someone to be born again against his will.

However, the family of Christ is what will exist forever. Thus, tragedy exists if a family member on earth refuses to convert. Those who belong to the family of Christ will be in Heaven with Christ forever, and those who do not belong to it will go to Hell, forever. Right now, if you have a non-Christian mother, you may be sad at the prospect. But in Heaven, we won't be bound to earthly ties. In fact, you will not feel sadness that your mother is not in Heaven. The Bible describes Christians as glorifying Jesus for sending people to the eternal holocaust in Hell. It almost seems heartless right now, but future reality will be different from the current reality.

Jesus gave a picture of this future reality in the New Testament. Biblical scholars call this "realized eschatology." When Jesus is told that His mother and brothers were waiting for Him, Jesus replied, "Who is my mother and who is my brother? Those who do the will of God." And we know that the will of God is that we believe in Jesus Christ and find salvation in Him. But we have free will. We can embrace Jesus or we can reject Jesus. It is up to each and everyone.

Jesus gave this seemingly heartless response to show the picture of the coming of the fullness of the Kingdom of Christ. In Heaven, those who belong to the family of Christ are our family members for eternity. If we see the eternal import of salvation in Christ, it is understandable why American Baptists are particularly very eager about converting family members and friends to Christ. Time is limited on earth, but in the future, eternity will be for eternity.

In a sense, we can say that these American Baptists are in tune with the reality of the Kingdom of Christ and its future implications. Given the dedication of American Baptists to this future reality, it's not surprising why American Baptists were successful in convincing people to accept Jesus Christ as their personal Savior (by the grace of Jesus Christ).

But for many around the world, the Kingdom of Christ may seem non-existent because it is not fully realized until the Second Coming of Jesus Christ. But just because you cannot see the Kingdom of Christ, it does not mean it does not exist. You can't see oxygen, but oxygen exists. Otherwise, you would not be able to breathe.

The Kingdom of Christ is very real, and it is important for us to think about the significance of belonging to that Kingdom. So, we ask again: What does it mean to be citizens in the Kingdom of

Christ? First and foremost obligation is to recognize that Jesus Christ is the King of kings and the LORD of lords. This may seem like stating the obvious, but it is the most important thing. We must recognize that Jesus Christ is the King of kings and the LORD of lords even when we are in our weakest moment.

Whether we are strong or whether we are ill, Christ is the King of kings and the LORD of lords. Jesus Christ is not only the King of kings when we are strong. The kingship of Christ is independent of our situation in life, experience, turmoils, happy moments, etc. Jesus Christ is always the King of kings and the LORD of lords. Being a citizen of the Kingdom of Christ obligates us to actively acknowledge this reality of the Kingship of Jesus Christ. This can be seen as the primary obligation of the citizen of the Kingdom of Christ.

Thus, thinking that Jesus Christ is the King of kings and the LORD of lords only when we are doing the "right" things is the wrong way to view our citizenship in the Kingdom of Christ. Jesus Christ is always the King of kings and the LORD of lords, when we do good as well as when we sin. We must emphasize the Kingship of Christ and openly acknowledge it at our strongest as well as at our weakest moments.

The second responsibility of the citizen of the Kingdom of Christ is to fulfill the Great Commission. The reason why the Great Commission is important is that Jesus Christ gave the Great Commission as a direct commandment for His followers, the citizens of His Kingdom. As long as the citizens of the Kingdom of Christ are living on earth, this responsibility should be at the forefront.

What does the Great Commission command? Christians are to proselytize non-Christians in our locale and even beyond national borders to the end of the world. In a sense, Jesus Christ defined the citizenship in the Kingdom of Christ as chiefly involving evangelism. Jesus as the King of kings and the LORD of lords came to earth to redeem all who would, out of their free will, accept Him as their King and LORD. Jesus gave Himself in a sacrificial death in order to grant the citizenship in the Kingdom of Christ. It is a very costly citizenship, but Jesus Christ is willing to give it freely to all those who would accept Him of free will.

In a sense, the Great Commission obligates all the citizens of the Kingdom of Christ to strategize together to carry out the Great Commission. In a sense, we can even say that Christian identity as a group is affirmed in the colluding together to convert as many non-Christians to Christianity. The more that Christians work together to fulfill the Great Commission, they affirm their partnership in the Kingdom of Christ. Citizens of the Kingdom of Christ will come together to fulfill the Great Commission.

Thus, not only is evangelism an obligation for the citizens of the Kingdom of Christ, it is an identity marker. In other words, a Christian is a Christian because she seeks to convert non-Christians to Christ. Conversely, a Christian who does not seek to convert non-Christian to Christ casts his Christian identity into doubt. This is a very important point to make.

Christian identity, opposed to Jewish identity, is not about keeping laws. Everything is secondary to the primary question of putting faith in the Kingship and the Lordship of Christ. To uphold Jesus as the Messiah marks an individual as a Christian. A Christian must emphasize that Jesus Christ is the King of kings and the LORD of lords in her strongest moment as well as at her weakest moment.

Evangelism is very important because it is a public proclamation of the Kingship and the Lordship of Jesus Christ. Why should others accept Jesus Christ as the Messiah? The answer is found in the fact that Jesus Christ is God and is the only one who can give membership in the Kingdom of Christ. Salvation is only through Jesus Christ, the King of kings and the LORD of lords. Evangelism for the Kingdom of God is akin to an American proclaiming, "I am an American!"

Evangelism affirms a Christian's membership in the Kingdom of Christ. It is important to remember the New Testament teaching: "All who profess with their mouth that Christ is LORD will be saved." It is necessary for Christians to emphasize that Jesus Christ is God. It is crucial for Christians to stress that Jesus is the King of kings and the LORD of lords who can grant membership in the Kingdom of Christ. It is important to proclaim to non-Christians the reality of the Kingdom of Christ and to encourage them to participate in the Kingdom. Fulfilling the Great Commission affirms our citizenship in the Kingdom of Christ.

The issue of fulfilling the Great Commission raises the question of effectiveness of evangelism and its relevance for the citizens of the Kingdom of Christ. How important is it that we are effective in converting others? I would emphatically state that it is very important. It is important to find effective methods to fulfill the Great Commission. If our method does not yield result, then other effective methods must be sought and found.

Jesus Christ emphasizes converting others to Christianity although He did not specify any particular method. What methods we use to convert others to Christ is not as important. It is important, however, that we find a very effective method to get the desired effect. The goal is to convert non-Christians to Christianity. We want non-Christians to choose out of their free will to accept Jesus Christ as the King of kings and the LORD of lords. It is important to find good strategies to get the maximum result, to convert as many people as possible to Christianity.

Thus, Christians are called to creative thinking and bold action. When we examine the methods Jesus Christ used to convert non-Christians to Christianity, we are impressed by the diversity of techniques employed. We are aware of Jesus sending out the twelve. Disciples of Jesus Christ were sent into villages to convert non-Christians to Christianity. Some Baptist Christians in America have followed this model and are found visiting houses with their Bible. Surprisingly, this method has proven quite effective, particularly with the elderly and homes with children. Often, Christians brought message of hope at the right time.

Of course, Christians visiting homes randomly in evangelism have no idea what each family needs. It would be safe to assume that the Holy Spirit is at work. God knows what people need. And when Christians actively engage in evangelism, God moves by His Spirit to bring the evangelist to the people who are in need and desire to find salvation. Obviously, if Christians are sitting at home, it would be difficult to get them to address the spiritual needs of non-Christians. Christians who are moving and going from door to door can be guided by the Spirit as they are more in tune with the Spirit.

Jesus employs other techniques in evangelism. The New Testament describes Jesus as performing miracles and drawing large crowds. Jesus used this opportunity to call people to faith in Him. Some Christians have copied this kind of evangelism technique. It is not surprising in some areas to find Christians performing a mime-dance or a type of magic show to draw crowds in public places. Then, these Christians share the message of the Christian Gospel.

Related to this technique is what many Christian Youth Groups in America do for evangelism. In the summer time, a group of people go to a non-Christian country or area and sing practiced Gospel songs. Then, an evangelist shares a short message. Testimonies after testimonies in American churches show that this type of evangelism technique has proven effective.

We must remember that Christianity is not a difficult religion. All people have to do is to accept Jesus Christ as the King of kings and the LORD of lords to be saved. Basically, if you believe Jesus Christ is God and confess with your mouth that Jesus is the King of kings, you automatically become a citizen of the Kingdom of Christ. It is that easy. The commitment can be made in a fraction of a minute. That is why it is important to make a call to commitment. Some American Baptists often make the call to commitment after every sermon. Protracting the call could actually hinder the commitment.

Jesus uses other methods in evangelism. Perhaps troubling to those of gentle disposition is the fact that Jesus often used bullying techniques to encourage non-Christians to make the Christian commitment. Jesus Christ often verbally abused Jewish religious leaders. Jesus called the Pharisees, "Hypocrites." And Jesus even cursed at them. Furthermore, Jesus incessantly dismissed the ideas of the Pharisees as incorrect or irrelevant. The New Testament often shows Jesus as disrespecting the Pharisees and the Sadducees. Jesus does not shy away from bullying techniques but embrace them. Of course, it must be emphasized that even with this technique, Jesus wanted His hearers to make the commitment out of their free will.

Jesus' bullying techniques are often downplayed among some Christian circles. Perhaps, this destroys the picture of Jesus as a gentle soul. But it cannot be denied that Jesus often plays the bully with Jewish religious leaders in the New Testament. In effect, Jesus legitimates bullying evangelism as a viable tool for effective evangelism. Bullying techniques have surprisingly been very effective in the history of Christianity in getting people to make the commitment to Jesus Christ out of their free will.

America's itinerant preachers preaching about Hell on street corners have converted thousands and thousands to Christianity. Jonathan Edward's sermon, "Sinners in the Hands of an Angry God," is a good example of a bully-type preaching. Such a technique in preaching is particularly found in American churches in the inner city and has proven effective even in converting hardened criminals to Christianity. Some Christians in America actually point to the reluctance of the

English evangelicals to use bullying preaching as a reason for the continuing demise of Christianity in the United Kingdom.

Whatever technique Christians decide to use, it is very important that Christians recognize the importance of effective evangelism. To be a citizen in the Kingdom of Christ centralizes the fulfillment of the obligations to the Great Commission of Jesus Christ. Participating in the Great Commission defines Christians as Christians. It is the evidence of the membership in the Kingdom of Christ.

Besides the active recognition of Jesus as the King of kings and the LORD of lords and a proactive participation in the Great Commission, citizenship in the Kingdom of Christ necessitates loyalty to the Kingdom of Christ. Not too many Christians would disagree with the statement that Christians need to be loyal to the Kingdom of Christ. However, unfortunately, Christians do not often think about what this really means. What does it mean to be loyal to the Kingdom of Christ? What does this mean in real terms? What does the loyalty to Christ involve in terms of our involvement in society and politics? As I feel that the topic of Christian loyalty requires extensive examination, I will devote the following chapters to the question.

Chapter 3:

Christian Loyalty and Political Obligation

It is not always easy to talk about a Christian's political responsibility. Many Christians disagree about politics and about various issues. For example, should Christians support raising income taxes or not? Some Christians believe that raising the income tax is good for the common good because it will make public funds available for more social services. Other Christians believe that raising the income tax is bad because it limits the spending capacity of the consumer which fuels economic growth and thereby contributes to the common good.

Perhaps, the best way to tackle the issue of Christian loyalty and political obligation is to focus on the larger questions, rather than individual issues. This is wise for several reasons. First of all, the example of the income tax noted above shows that there are individual issues that are more or less "neutral" when it comes to the question of Christian loyalty and political obligation. Whether a Christian supports the raising of the income tax or not, it will not typically have a bearing on the Kingdom of Christ (unless there are other larger issued tied to it). Secondly, there are a lot of issues. It is practically impossible to address every issue that faces Christians in the political realm. And new issues rise all the time. It is better to talk about larger principles that can guide decision making on individual issues. Thirdly, focusing on the larger questions helps Christians to develop a coherent world view. Understanding what is a Christian way to understand the world helps the Christian understand not only her obligations in the realm of politics but in other areas as well.

How should the Christian understand Christian loyalty in the realm of politics? Simply put, Christians should privilege the Kingdom of Christ over any other political loyalty. This should be the guiding principle. This is the answer to the "larger question." Whenever Christians are faced with the question of who to be more loyal to, Christians must choose the Kingdom of Christ over any other obligation or association.

In a sense, loyalty to the Kingdom of Christ presupposes the possibility of conflict. It is important for Christians to recognize that such a conflict is possible and prepare for it. The fact is that the Kingdom of Christ is a kingdom with a king and a set of laws. Jesus Christ, the King of kings, demands absolute loyalty. Thus, when a Christian who lives in an earthly kingdom, whether that be the United Kingdom, the USA, or any other country, faces the question of loyalty, she must choose the Kingdom of Christ.

Loyalty to the Kingdom of Christ is more easily stated as a principle and more difficult to see in the context of reality. I will endeavor to show how the principle should be applied in reality. The best way to start the discussion is by using an example. If a Christian is a Senator and is voting on the question of abortion, she must vote against it. It does not matter if her political party supports abortion; she must be more loyal to the Kingdom of Christ.

Recently, the Pope emphasized that no Catholic priest should administer mass to Catholics who vote for abortion. Obviously, a person has the right to be a Catholic or not. A person is free to choose what she wants. But if a person chooses to be a Catholic, she places herself under the religious authority of the Catholic Church. Catholic priests have the right to refuse communion to Catholics who violate Catholic laws. No one is putting a gun to the Catholic politician to remain a Catholic.

The proclamation by the pope highlights the obligations of a Christian in the political realm. Obviously, a politician can be Christian or convert to another religion. But as long as a politician remains – out of her own will – to be a Christian, she is under obligations to the Kingdom of Christ.

Thus, a Christian Senator must vote to support the Kingdom of Christ in policy decisions. Obviously, there are issues, like taxes, which are less relevant in terms of being loyal to the Kingdom of Christ. But issues like abortion are quite clear cut. A Christian Senator, as long as she remains a Christian, must vote against abortion. Ireland is one Christian country that has made abortion illegal. America's Christians, who are some 80% of the population, would be content with an anti-abortion law, such as the one that exists in Ireland. The biggest problem is that legal history has made it difficult to overturn abortion laws.

This shows that the question of Christian loyalty is not confined to the Senate chambers. As the American government is divided into the executive, the legislative, and the judiciary, it is important to emphasize that all who participate in any of the parts of the government are obligated to be loyal to Christ in their position at work. Thus, a judge in the US court system must find ways to uphold the Christian law against abortion. In other words, Christian judges must find ways to overturn the abortion law in the legal realm. This is particularly important in light of the fact that the judiciary prevents anti-abortion laws and policies from being passed.

Also in the area of the judiciary, lawyers must get involved in fighting abortion. There are lawyers who grease the system of laws at every level and at every place. A Christian lawyer, wherever she is in her level and expertise, should make a concerted effort to overturn pro-abortion laws. It is only by the activation of every Christian and her awareness of her responsibility that positive changes can be made.

In the USA, such movements are gaining greater momentum. More and more Christian lawyers are getting involved in fighting pro-abortion laws. Particularly the younger generation of Christian lawyers is dedicated to overturning the laws. A part of the reason for this reality is that younger generation of Christians has a reformed understanding of the question of the relationship between the Church and the State.

In the past generation, lawyers understood the separation of Church and State as pushing out of the legal system anything that may be favorable to Christian principles. Certainly, the original intention of the separation of the Church and the State was to protect the Church from the invasion of the State. But the developed interpretation of the separation between the Church and the State principle has taken a wrong turn somewhere down the line.

Given the fact that the majority of Americans are Christians and oppose abortion makes it seem odd that abortion laws are protected by extreme legal gymnastics. In this light, the misappropriation of the separation of the Church and the State principle to uphold abortion laws seem grossly outdated and unfair in light of the representative principle of democracy. The suppression of the majority of Americans by a misinterpreted principle smacks of fascism more than anything else.

Just as Christians in the legislative and judiciary branches of the government must privilege the Kingdom of Christ over any other loyalties, the Christian in the executive branch of government must privilege Christian loyalty over all else. Thus, a Christian President must veto any legislation that go against the Kingdom of Christ. More importantly, the President must proactively support Christian principles.

President George W. Bush has been pretty good about supporting Christian principles. President Bush is particularly popular among Americans because he supports Christian principles openly. Everyone is aware of the active anti-abortion position that President George W. Bush has taken. To the surprise of many political pundits, President Bush's open support of anti-abortion legislation has won political support. However, I am not suggesting that President Bush is using this as a political ploy to gain further support. It seems that President Bush's anti-abortion position seems genuinely from the heart.

Certainly, it is important for Christian policymakers in the executive, the legislative, and the judiciary branches of the government to be loyal to the Kingdom of Christ and act according to their primary loyalty.

President George W. Bush has made a public confession of his Christian faith and its bearing on him as a person and as a policymaker. But I don't think that all Christians necessarily have to be so overt. It is better to be overt than not. However, it is possible that closet Christians can do a lot to change laws and policies to support the Kingdom of Christ. While I would object to denying Christian identity, downplaying it in order to produce concrete pro-Christian decisions in a hostile environment may, in fact, be a good strategy. The important thing is to push pro-Christian legislation and policy. Being effective to do this is what's most important.

The case of abortion laws shows the important roles that Christians in the executive, the legislative, and the judiciary play. However, it is not only policymakers who are important. Ordinary citizens, who are not in policy making positions, can also play an important role in affecting abortion legislation. In fact, ordinary citizens are obligated to show their loyalty to the Kingdom of Christ as much as Christian policymakers are. The question should be in the how.

What roles can ordinary Christians play to privilege Christian loyalty on the issue of abortion? The history of anti-abortion struggles indicates that ordinary citizens have already played important roles in this regard. The most notable is the organization skills employed by various Christian leaders and laity (mostly among the Catholics and the Baptists) to mobilize grassroots opposition to abortion legislation.

Ordinary Americans will not be surprised to receive phone calls or mails providing information and seeking voluntary support for anti-abortion policies. Retired persons and the disabled often show themselves as leaders in spearheading some anti-abortion policies. People who do not seem like they can be leaders transform themselves into effective links in the anti-abortion campaign at the grassroots level. Some youths even design anti-abortion websites and lend their technological know-how to getting the anti-abortion message across the internet.

Ordinary Americans have marched in anti-abortion rallies, signed petitions, contacted government leaders, and organized church functions to oppose abortion. Now, practically every state in the USA has an active anti-abortion campaign with full-time staff to keep watch on policy making at the local, state, and federal levels. The anti-abortion movement, therefore, can be seen as a success story of grassroots mobilization.

It is becoming increasingly clear that ordinary Americans have forced themselves into political discourse. Now, these ordinary Americans cannot be ignored. Over the years, ordinary Americans involved in anti-abortion campaigns have become increasingly sophisticated and even successfully enlisted businesses and political leaders. American politicians know that taking an active anti-abortion position will mean real votes, particularly from Catholic and Baptist Christians.

The genius of the grassroots anti-abortion movement, therefore, can be seen in the functional way they have asserted themselves in the political process. They are not just one of many voices that do not matter. They are a voice that matters.

They have been able to mobilize the masses to vote for candidates who oppose abortion, so they have a real political pull. Having massive membership and the ability to mobilize votes compel both those politicians who actually oppose abortion or just want votes to win to consider the anti-abortion campaign seriously.

Thus, functionally, the grassroots anti-abortion campaigns get concrete policy votes from elected official to oppose abortion. The record on abortion voting is published publicly. And many American Christians will vote against a candidate just based on their abortion legislation voting record.

In contrast, British anti-abortion movements have not been well-organized. There are organizations, but it would be difficult to find people in British churches that have even made a 5 pound contribution to any of these anti-abortion campaigns. The reality is vastly different in the USA. In a given church, it is easy to find people who have made monetary contributions as well as those who have participated in the anti-abortion campaign personally (such as in rallies or volunteer work).

Also, British anti-abortion movements have been utterly unsuccessful in compelling any politician to vote against abortion. Perhaps, it's the idealistic approach that the British take. British anti-abortion lobbies seem to take a "moral" high ground and appeal to reason. Of course, most politicians do not listen to reason. Since the beginning of the history of humankind, rarely have politicians listened to reason. Ideals of Enlightenment do not seem to jive with the reality of the political process.

In contradistinction to the British idealism, American anti-abortion movement appeals to the reality. And the politician can be voted out of office. If the politician does not vote against abortion, he is punished in print and in rallies. There is aggressiveness about the way pro-abortion politicians are attacked. It may be possible to call this a type of bullying tactic. But this seems to produce desired results in many cases in the USA or come very close to it.

Other ways ordinary Americans have become involved in trying to push anti-abortion legislation is by more indirect route. Instead of joining anti-abortion groups and working with them directly, some ordinary American Christians get involved in the local political party. For instance, they volunteer to help a candidate win a political election. In the process of volunteering their time and getting in the political process, they try to sway the camp towards a more anti-abortion position.

This type of involvement can be seen as "subversive." And often young college students volunteer in political campaigns with this strategy in mind. American Christians are taught from elementary school years that abortion is opposed to Christianity. This ingrained understanding of abortion as something that should be illegalized affects many American college students as they get involved in the political process. The fact that Catholic and Baptist ministries are very active on many college campuses shows that there is an infrastructure to support anti-abortion movement at the university level.

It is no surprise, therefore, that Ralph Reed, a very active Christian, became a political strategist for key anti-abortion candidates. Reed is seen as a political strategist and effective at subversion so that an anti-abortion candidate can actually win. Reed is not the only one who became actively involved in the political process in college years. There are literally thousands of people like him, and many of them see overturning pro-abortion laws as a priority.

Ralph Reed as well as other Christians who get involved in the political process desire to be loyal to Christ and His Kingdom. The concept of the Kingdom of Christ is particularly important among the Catholics and the Baptists, so it's not surprising that they produce the most involved Christian activists.

It is important to see that their involvement against abortion represents their loyalty to the Kingdom of Christ. They are privileging the Kingdom of Christ over and against any other loyalty. Pro-abortion laws currently exist in the USA. The courts are sworn to uphold these pro-abortion laws. The police are employed to guard these pro-abortion laws. Thus, when Christians oppose these pro-abortion laws, they are in essence making a Christian statement. They rather oppose American laws that go against the Law of Christ.

The example of abortion illustrates what it means for Christians to be loyal to the Kingdom of Christ in the political realm. As a matter of principle, for Christians to be loyal to the Kingdom of Christ will necessarily mean opposing current laws. In other words, if Britain has an anti-Christian law or regulation that limits Christianity, Christians must not respect these laws. Upholding a British law just because it is a law is tantamount to being a traitor to the Kingdom of Christ when the law violates Christianity. Law is not in and of itself sacred.

This is an important point to emphasize. Law is not the standard of human morality or the guideline for human behavior. We have to remember what laws have done in modern times. Hitler passed a law to kill 6 million Jews. Killing Jews was perfectly legal. In fact, not killing Jews was illegal. A soldier who refused to arrest Jews to kill them was violating an instituted state law and could go to jail. Putting aside the question of whether it was God's punishment of Jews that the Holocaust happened, it is important to recognize that the law upheld the killing of Jews. It was legal. It had the support of the government. Police agencies were forced to uphold this law. Soldiers were obligated to fight for this law.

Hitler's law, which was perfectly legal and legitimate under a sovereign nation, highlights the fallacy of law. American Christians, more than British Christians, therefore, take a more critical view of law and its impact on society. British Christians have been complacent and passive in accepting laws in place. While Christianity Today chronicles many efforts by American Christians to change laws, no such serious efforts seem to be found in Britain. American churches often preach against abortion, but one will be hard-pressed to find a British clergyman preach against abortion. American churches tend to recognize the supremacy of the Kingdom of Christ implicitly, but British churches seem to relegate the Kingdom of Christ under the United Kingdom.

Another example of how legal process was tainted is in the way the Jews tried to have Jesus Christ suffer the capital punishment. Currently, the State of Israel issues capital punishment to one group of people. The enemies of the Jews suffer capital punishment. Thus, the Nazis are put to death. But it's not only the Nazis. The State of Israel feels that it had the right to kill anyone whom it deems as "the enemy of the Jews." Likewise, in the Second Temple period, Jewish leaders identified Jesus Christ as "the enemy of the Jews." Rightly so, because Jesus hated Judaism and constantly attacked Jewish purity laws. Jesus threatened to destroy the Jewish Temple. Jesus cursed at Jewish religious leaders. Jesus emphasized that salvation is only through Him and that Jewish legal observance was useless. Jesus bullied Jewish leaders and disrespected Judaism. Jews were right to think of Jesus as the enemy of Judaism.

And as today's Jews are willing to kill the "threat" to Jews, Jews at Jesus' time were willing to kill Jesus Christ. Jews were concerned about the law, so they desired to kill Jesus according to the Jewish law. Jews tell Jesus that Jesus must die according to the Jewish laws. In the Gospel of John, the High Priest of the Jewish Temple persuaded the Jewish leaders to have Jesus killed. All the while, Jewish leaders were looking for legal ways to actually kill Jesus. They were concerned about official legal process but were willing to "play dirty." The Gospels describe Jews as constantly trying to entrap Jesus at his word.

The Pharisees seem to send out spies to record Jesus' actions and to find some "dirt" to pin on Jesus. Not only that, Jewish leaders try to produce false witnesses and testimonials that is distorting the facts so that they can be used against Jesus Christ in the court of law. The Jewish leaders are concerned about legal procedure and want to convict Jesus through legitimate court process. Behind the scenes, Jews do all they can to tip the verdict in their favor. The case of Jesus must raise critical questions regarding the law for Christians. British Christians do bear the blame for moral weakness in their blind support of "law and order." It was "law and order" that compelled the Jews to kill Jesus Christ.

It is not surprising, therefore, that Christian writers from St. Augustine and Thomas Aquinas to John Calvin and Martin Luther recognized the supremacy of the Kingdom of Christ and the subjugation of all earthly laws and powers under Christ.

Law, in and of itself, is not good. Law is not necessarily moral. In fact, the above example shows that law and legal process are often evil. Jesus Christ taught this in the New Testament, and Christians must take this more to heart. Christians, after the example of Jesus Christ, must distrust all laws implicitly. Laws must be questioned in light of the Christian obligation to the Kingdom of Christ.

Thus, if a law adversely affects the Kingdom of Christ, it must be opposed. Not only a law that is not yet passed should be opposed but also a law that has already been passed. Just like American policy makers who are Christians are working to overturn pro-abortion laws, British Christians must work to repeal anti-Christian laws currently in place in the United Kingdom. No Christian is under the authority of British Law when it opposes Christ. Christians are, first and foremost, citizens of the

Kingdom of Christ. Christian loyalty to Christ always supercedes loyalty to the United Kingdom.

The obligation to be loyal is not confined to leaders alone. Ordinary citizens must remain loyal to the Kingdom of Christ. Thus, British Christians have an obligation to resist evil in the form of laws that are anti-Christian. British Christians are not obligated to keep the laws that oppose the Kingdom of Christ. In fact, observing British laws that oppose the Kingdom of Christ represents rebellion against the Kingdom of Christ. In other words, when British Christians actively observe British laws that are anti-Christian, British Christians in effect have made an active decision to rebel against the Kingdom of Christ. Active rebellion against the Kingdom of Christ is a serious matter that will not be treated lightly by Jesus Christ, the King of kings and the LORD of lords. Treason is a serious violation in any nation, and it is no different with the Kingdom of Christ.

Christians are obligated not to rebel against the Kingdom of Christ. Christians must not commit treason against the Kingdom of Christ. When the United Kingdom decides to pass anti-Christian laws and force its citizens to observe them, British Christians must resist evil. Observing British law is rebellion and treason against the Kingdom of Christ. It is better to commit treason against the United Kingdom and support the Kingdom of Christ. Treason against United Kingdom only has temporal consequences, but the treason against the Kingdom of Christ has eternal consequences.

In other words, if the British government imprisons British Christians for violating anti-Christian laws, it should be a source of pride for British Christians. British Christians have proven that they are more loyal to Christ, the King of kings and the LORD of lords. Not opposing anti-Christian laws in order to save oneself should be a source of shame for British Christians. As Jesus Christ said, "Those who will try to save their life will lose it, but those who lose their life for my sake will save it." British Christians must particularly take the warning of Jesus Christ to heart as the United Kingdom is passing directly anti-Christian laws.

Perhaps, it may be helpful to describe how Christians in the British context can resist evil in the form of anti-Christian laws being passed in the United Kingdom. First of all, British Christians can actively oppose it. If the United Kingdom states that it is illegal to say that Jesus Christ is the only Savior and those who do not believe in Jesus will go to Hell, then British Christians must go out of their way to preach this on Sunday worship services and print the statement in church bulletins and publiccations. This is an active resistance of evil. Silence is tantamount to participation in the evil – anti-Christian laws.

Silence means rebellion against the Kingdom of Christ. When the United Kingdom passes clearly anti-Christian laws, it is a direct assault on the Kingdom of Christ and Jesus Christ, the King of kings and the LORD of lords. British Christians are obligated to defend the honor of Christ and the sanctity of the Kingdom of Christ. British Christians must actively resist evil.

Secondly, British Christians can organize a campaign to have these laws overturned. For instance, the Christian Union and Fusion cellgroups across the United Kingdom can organize petition signing drives and send letters to local

MP's. Attractive tracts can be made making people (first of all, Christians) aware of the anti-Christian laws and their implications. Talks can be held discussing the details of the laws, which government officials support these policies, and the future direction of similar legislation. The campaign will involve both raising of awareness among Christians and an effort to overturn anti-Christian laws. Individual Christians involved in this campaign can write letters directly to their political leaders and also contact local newspapers and radio stations.

Thirdly, ordinary citizens can try to subvert from within. For instance, British Christians who are already in the system, whether in the political or legal, can try to sway the official (but more importantly unofficial) discourse towards the overturning of already decided laws. It is important to sway opinions of policy makers. More often than not, most people do not feel strongly one way or another about any given issue. British Christians do not do enough to sway the vast majority of people in any given setting who can be swayed with a little bit of concerted effort.

For instance, if a Christian is working on the staff of a MP from Oxfordshire, she can try to find ways to sway the opinions of those in the office and even the MP herself to a more pro-Christian stance. Obviously, methods and intensity will vary based on the situation and the candidate. But a Christian who is in that place of work is there for a (divine) reason. She must not deny her responsibility to the Kingdom of Christ. She cannot remain silent. Silence is tantamount to rebellion against the Kingdom of Christ.

Another example can be found with a lawyer in the British system. Whichever place the lawyer occupies in the British legal system, she can play her part to overturn anti-Christian legislation. Many of the legal discussions will touch relevant issues that have a bearing on anti-Christian legislation. She must find ways to contribute in the short-run and in the long-run to overturning anti-Christian decisions that have far-reaching conesquences. There are more than a few Christian lawyers in the British legal system. If they put even a little bit of their brain power and effort, collectively their individual efforts will be strong and can affect positive changes.

Unfortunately, however, British Christians remain silent. When it comes to anti-Christian decisions, silence is tantamount to rebellion against the Kingdom of Christ. Christian lawyers are obligated to play subversive roles where laws are meant to be anti-Christian. Christian lawyers' primary obligation is to the Kingdom of Christ, and not to the United Kingdom.

While it is important to emphasize that Christians already in the system must oppose anti-Christian decisions actively or from behind the scenes, it is further important to stress the need to encourage Christians to infiltrate systems with the sole goal of overturning anti-Christian decisions. How can Christians infiltrate?

Christians who graduate from college can make it their personal goal (and plan) to get involved in the political process. It can be in the form of volunteering spare time in political party activities. Christians would not have to alter their work patterns as many political party meetings are available in the evenings and on weekends. As Christians become more involved in political party programs, they will have opportunities to give their input. When Christians plan seriously and try to find ways to influence outcome more favorable to Christianity, a real change can be made.

More well-to-do Christian college students, especially if they have the support of their Christian parents, may actually consider working full-time for a couple of years in a political party or a political organization. Working full-time without worries as to the repercussions to finances is a benefit for college graduates from wealthy families. It is not a bad idea to put God-given wealth to use to advance the Kingdom of Christ in the political realm. In fact, this is one way wealthy Christian college graduates can show their genuine appreciation to Jesus Christ for the wealth that they have been given by the grace of Jesus Christ, the King of kings and the LORD of lords.

But not only wealthy college students should work full time for political organizations. Although missing a type of safety net, college Christians can commit to working for political organizations with the goal of pushing more pro-Christian legislation. It will be more like being a domestic Christian missionary. There are risks to be sure but Christians can test their faith in Jesus Christ if they opt to dive into the water without a safety net.

Why is working full-time in a political organization akin to being a domestic missionary? The fact is that preponderance of anti-Christian legislation hinders effective Christian evangelism and work. It is far better and easier to spread the Good News under favorable conditions than hostile ones. Instead of leaving political and social conditions to "chance," Christians working full-time can direct legislation that's favorable to Christianity. More importantly, Christians working full-time in political groups could "subvert" their organizations in order to overturn anti-Christian legislation already in place and in effect. This "paving" work is far more significant to Christian evangelism than we give credit for. Bright college graduates must expand their horizon of thinking about evangelism and use the skills they have acquired in college directly in the area of politics.

Thus far, the discussion of Christian loyalty in the political realm involved discussion of overturning anti-Christian decisions. The reason that this was first discussed is that this is of the greatest consequence in the political realm. For, it is impossible to talk about loyalty without talking about conflicting loyalties.

When we say that Christians as the citizens of the Kingdom of Christ must be loyal, first and foremost, to the Kingdom of Christ, we are necessarily saying that Christians must be disloyal to other obligations. When there is a conflict of loyalties between the Kingdom of Christ and the United Kingdom (for example), it is impossible to be loyal to both. Christians must betray one (at least around the issues involved) and be loyal to the other. Christians must choose the Kingdom of Christ. Choosing the United Kingdom in such a case is tantamount to choosing against the Kingdom of Christ.

It is important to think seriously about the exclusive nature of loyalty. Even Jesus Christ emphasized that you cannot have two masters. You have to serve the one and hate the other. You have to choose. Jesus Christ, in effect, laid down the principle of the exclusive nature of loyalty. Obviously, Jesus expected wise ones to choose Jesus over everything else, but that always was not the case. Jews have stated that they have eyes but they do not see and that they have ears but they do not hear.

Jesus was criticizing the Jewish leaders for not choosing Jesus over the Jewish law. Jewish leaders saw Jesus every day and perceived what he did. But they did not really see in the sense that they did not choose wisely according to what Jesus demanded of them. Jewish leaders heard what Jesus said. They were inundated with His message of love and salvation, but they did not really understand. Obviously, they did not make the wise decision based on what they heard. For Jesus Christ, the Jewish leaders' inability to choose wisely was evidence for their dumbness and blindness. It mattered little that they saw and heard all; they still made the bad decision that had grave consequences for themselves, their family, and their people.

The principle of loyalty as outlined by Jesus Christ was an all-or-nothing proposition. You choose Jesus Christ over all and receive the benefits of the Kingdom of Christ. Or you choose against Jesus Christ and receive the judgments targeted at the enemies of Jesus Christ. Some may find the all-or-nothing proposition somewhat disturbing, but the fact is that this is the way Jesus taught loyalty to the Kingdom of Christ.

It is because of the all-or-nothing loyalty to the Kingdom of Christ that many Christians in history have been martyred. Many Christians willingly were killed for their Christian faith because they chose to be more loyal to the Kingdom of Christ. In fact, loyalty to the point of giving up one's life is an emphasized virtue in the Christian faith. Since the very beginning, Christians were called to be loyal to Jesus Christ to the point of death. Thus, it is no surprise that many of the earliest disciples were killed for their Christian faith.

Take for example the story of St. Stephen in the Book of Acts. St. Stephen was a Christian and loyal to Jesus Christ. Therefore, Jewish leaders pursued him in order to kill him. Stephen had to choose between Judaism and Christianity. If Stephen chose Judaism, then he would have been allowed to live. If Stephen chose Christianity, he would be killed.

We all know the story. St. Stephen chose the Kingdom of Christ over Judaism and Jews killed him for it. The story of Stephen is a good example of what it means to be loyal to the Kingdom of Christ. It is more than possible that on earth Christians can get killed for their loyalty to Jesus Christ and His Kingdom. But Christians as citizens of the Kingdom of Christ are obligated to be loyal to Jesus Christ, the King of kings and the LORD of lords.

And Jesus Christ rewards those who are loyal to Him. St. Stephen saw Jesus Christ sitting at the right hand of God. St. Stephen was indeed going over to join the King of kings and the LORD of lords. As the Kingdom of Christ is forever, the choice was the right one to make. It is better to spend eternity in Heaven at the full realization of the Kingdom of Christ at the Second Coming of Christ than to suffer eternally in Hell. Christians have often understood that there is a special crown of righteousness reserved for those who suffer martyrdom. The idea is that those who give their lives in committed loyalty to Jesus Christ have made the greatest testimony of their faith in Christ.

Christians have often described martyrdom as a gift of God. There is understanding that not all those who desire to die for the name of Jesus Christ, the King of kings and the LORD of lords will get their wish. There are many stories of Christians praying to have the honor of dying for the Kingdom of Christ. Even though many Christians remain loyal to the Kingdom of Christ to the end, they do not necessarily suffer martyrdom. Although not all succeed in dying for Jesus Christ, it is important to have the spirit of martyrdom. It is the Christian ideal to be willing to die for Christ. Loyalty to Christ at all cost is certainly something to strive for.

It is important to have an accurate understanding of exclusive loyalty to Jesus Christ. More often than not, Christians will face decisions in the political realm. If the Christian is not mentally, psychologically, and spiritually prepared to handle the conflict of loyalties, she will most likely falter. The temptation is against the Kingdom of Christ as we live in the world filled with sin.

In fact, Jesus described the world as the domain of Satan until the Second Coming when He will come as Judge and Executioner. Until the return of the Son of Man, the earth is a domain of sin and Satan. Unprepared, the Christian will necessaryly choose loyalty going against Christ. It is not easy being loyal to the Kingdom of Christ in this world.

It is only by being mentally, psychologically, and spiritually being prepared that Christians can spurn the wiles of the world and deceptions that try to entrap us. We can easily be led astray and made to falter.

Loyalty to Christ becomes further difficult because decisions are not made in a vacuum. It is not just you with two set of impersonal choices. It is not merely choosing between the two. Everyone is bound by social context and human relations. More often than not, these play critical roles in the decisions that we make. And in most cases people will try to manipulate your social context and human relations.

I would call this the crisis of loyalty because you are on the verge of making a decision and there are many forces pulling you in the wrong direction. You may, in your heart, want to make the decision to be loyal to Jesus Christ and perhaps you will if your decision was made in a vacuum. But your decision becomes complicated when social context and human relations are manipulated to push you towards being unfaithful to Jesus Christ.

For instance, you may have a non-Christian brother or father who is pressuring you to vote against the Kingdom of Christ. It is difficult to be loyal to the Kingdom of Christ, when one or more of your family members are not interested in upholding the interest of the Kingdom of Christ. They may genuinely support anti-Christian legislations and want you to join them. Perhaps, they see a rejection of anti-Christian legislation as a rejection of them. It is possible that they want an accomplice to a crime and it is crucial that you bloody your hand in the affair as well. Whatever may be the reason, one or more of your social relations can pressure you to be anti-Christian. You can be misguided to make the wrong decision and be disloyal to Jesus Christ.

Especially in the context of the reality that this world is the domain of Satan until Jesus Christ comes back again, it is possible to see that Satan can actually play a role in the spiritual realm in compelling you to make the wrong decision. Satan can manipulate your social relations to make you stumble. This is more likely than not if you are to believe in the words of Jesus that the world is in conflict. There is a real spiritual conflict and you can be made a pawn in the spiritual warfare. Your betrayal of Jesus Christ can have lasting consequences. Of course, for victory, Satanic forces will bombard you with all they have. It would be far easier to do as they wish than go against their pressure. As independent as you may think you are, you find yourself a prisoner of social relations. It takes a gargantuan amount of courage to resist, but most people lack that.

The higher up you are on the social ladder, it is more difficult to resist social pressure. The higher you go up on the social ladder, social relations are more regimented. There are perceived social obligations that your relations can manipulate to extort your commitment. In the process of making the wrong decision, not only do you make the wrong decision, but you lose a large part of yourself – who you are. As a citizen of Jesus Christ's Kingdom, you know that your loyalty lies with Jesus. However, Jesus' Kingdom is invisible. In a sense, you have the promise of the coming fulfillment of the Kingdom of Christ. But this promise does not feel tangible. It's something that cannot be seen. It is at a future time that the Kingdom of Christ will be realized in full glory with Christ visibly present as the King of kings and the LORD of lords.

On earth, what feels real is your social relations. People whom you see everyday are tangible and they are really there. What they say matters because you see them and hear them. You don't want them to dislike you. And when they try to make you feel guilty, the feelings of guilt seems real. Your sense of right and wrong becomes skewed in the midst of all the words that are being thrown at you. Just like a boxer is hit silly on a rink and he becomes dazed and confused, you become confused as people trying to push you toward the wrong decision. Even though you had made the decision to do right, your decisions feel wrong as your social relations bombard you.

The higher up the social ladder, it becomes difficult to make the decision of loyalty to the Kingdom of Christ. Non-Christian social relations will pull you away from Christ. In this light, it is understandable why Jesus said that it is difficult for a rich man to enter the Kingdom of Heaven like it is for a camel to go through the eye of a needle. It is not just the question of being tied to wealth. Rather, wealthy people are often bound by social relations. In a sense, social relations can be a part of the wealth system.

Because a person on a higher social ladder is entrapped by social relations more than ordinary people, it is more difficult for her to make the right decision. She feels obligated to take the recommendations of people seriously. And generally it is those who want her to make the wrong decisions that are more audible and visible. It is a tragedy of humanity that people that want a person to make the right decision remain invisible.

There may be several reasons for this. First of all, maybe some of her social relations want to see her fall. For instance, if a cousin married a third-rate man, she may want to see her cousin marry a third-rate man. It is, in part, jealousy. Furthermore, the cousin may fear that if she marries a man who is recognized by others as first-rate, her own standing would be decreased. It is probably true. If a woman is married to a third-rate man and her cousin is married to a first-rate man, the one with the first-rate man will generally enjoy higher import in society.

In the same way, a social relation may want to see you make the decision against Christ. Since they know how you feel about the Kingdom of Christ, their successful effort to choose something inferior will necessarily downgrade your status. They know that you have chosen against the first choice and they know that this will lose respect for you in the eyes of your peers in the long-run.

Generally, people have a respect for someone who sticks by her gun. If she has made a statement of loyalty to the Kingdom of Christ, the fact that she is able to resist any gestures and pressures to pull her away from her primary loyalty will win her respect. People have a saying that that they respect enemies who can't be swayed. How much more so those in your camp! They may resent you for choosing the Kingdom of Christ and not making the wrong decision (in the larger scheme of things), but they will view you as a woman of character. In the future, they may rely on you for leadership or trust because they know that you can't be easily manipulated. Decision against them will most likely be a credit to you. They will see you as a strong woman.

However, if you do what they want and betray Christ, then they will learn not to trust you. They will see you as easily manipulatable. They know that you will go where they want you to go. They know that you will do what they want you to do. They will see you as an easy person who can easily be manipulated. Your unfaithfulness to the

Kingdom of Christ (as much as they may want you to be) will prove you as a weakling in their eyes. When matters of temporal nature come up where they need to confide in someone, they will be less likely to trust you. They remember how easy it was to manipulate you, and they will fear that you may so easily be manipulated. They saw what you did. They remembered what they said to make you go away from your loyalty to the Kingdom of Christ. Thus, in real terms, your decision against the Kingdom of Christ is a decision against yourself, whether you see that now or not.

In the context of the upper class, it is easy to see how a person can forfeit her place in the Kingdom of Christ and also her place in her society. If she remained loyal to Christ, not being swayed to do against her real wish, at least she can maintain a place of respect. But higher you go up in the social ladder, more people want to see you fall. Especially if a cousin made a mistake in marrying a third rate man (so to speak), she may make it her primary business to make sure that you falter as well. In the context of respect and honor, making you to make the decision against the Kingdom of Christ may represent such an effort.

It is important to decide for the Kingdom of Christ in terms of long-term benefit on earth. The more important point is that it is the right thing to do. It is right, as the citizen of the Kingdom of Christ, not to go against the will of Jesus Christ. It is right on the cosmic plain. It is right on the Christian ethical plain.

Making the right decision in the cosmic order of things is essential. In order to succeed, you have to prepare mentally, psychologically, and spiritually. Without the inner strength, social relations and social context will cause you to stumble and make the wrong decision every time. We do not live in the realm of the realized Kingdom of Christ. We live in the hope of realization. We look to the future time of fulfillment. But it is crucial to remain loyal to the Kingdom of Christ, here and now.

It is, therefore, no surprise that Jesus Christ warns that many will fall away. St. Paul exhorts not to look to the right or to the left but straight at the goal ahead. The New Testament is filled with warning against making the wrong decision. The New Testament anticipates that the pressure to falter is stronger than the pressure to stay loyal. It is, indeed, very important to overcome the crisis of loyalty and be loyal to the Kingdom of Christ.

It is important to consider another factor. It is not merely our social relations and social contacts who want us to be disloyal to the Kingdom of Christ. There will be active supporters of anti-Christian legislation who want to pull us way from our Christian commitment. There is a reason why anti-Christian legislations were passed and put in place. There are those who truly desire anti-Christian situation to persist and advance. These anti-Christian pundits will not stop. It's like an engulfing fire that consumes them. They do all they can to pass more anti-Christian legislation. They are willing to destroy anyone who wants to oppose anti-Christian legislation. There is a snowballing effect once series of anti-Christian laws start being passed. This has proven to be the case, time and time again. And slowly all Christian lives, both those who actively resist or passively exist, become endangered.

Loyalty to the Kingdom of Christ

In the context of rising anti-Christian sentiment, it is important to emphasize the value of fighting fire with fire. Complacency is weakness. Appeasement will sound the death knell. In the wake of rising anti-Christianity, the only thing to do is strike back and strike back hard with significant consequences.

Some may ask the question of whether it is legitimate to strike back at the anti-Christian camp. Some may point to the concept of turning the other cheek as a reason not to strike back. More often than not, it is the non-Christian who points to the principle of turning the other cheek. Of course, it suits him to point to this principle so that he can overtake Christians in a conflict. If the non-Christian's purpose is to defeat Christians, it is good for him that weapons are taken away from Christians. Christians can be slaughtered without any resistance. Anti-Christian legislation can be passed again and again without a peep from the Christians.

It is important to recognize that the turning-the-other-cheek principle is one of the most misunderstood ideas from the Bible. Jesus clearly did not mean that we should let evil overtake us. Jesus certainly did not mean not fighting those who are anti-Christian. Jesus emphasized resisting evil. And even by example, Jesus fought evil.

In the Bible, Jesus calls the Jews, "Children of the Devil." Jesus pictures himself and his disciples in conflict with Jews and Judaism. Jesus said, "If you are not for us, then you are against us." In the New Testament, Jesus is found fighting with the Pharisees and Jewish teachers of the Law. At no point, does Jesus turns the other cheek. Jesus is verbally abusive towards Jewish leaders. In light of the fact that Jesus fought Jews and Judaism, it is safe to assume that turning the other cheek does not mean not resisting evil. Jesus' example clearly shows that it is important to strike back and even in cruel, bullying ways for the sake of righteousness.

From St. Augustine to modern Christian thinkers, most Christians intellectually support the right to resist evil. In other words, most Christian leaders support striking back at evil. It is important to resist evil because Christians are children of light. And light cannot be hidden. It must not be hidden.

The New Testament often uses fighting imagery. Christians are soldiers of Christ. Christians must put on the full armor of Christ. There is a spiritual sword. Christians are often depicted as spiritual warriors in conflict with evil. Our allegeance is to Jesus Christ, the King of kings and the LORD of lords.

It is clear that Christians have an obligation to resist evil. Anti-Christian legislation represents a great evil that must be resisted. Christians must not turn the other cheek in resisting evil. We must do as Jesus taught us and strike back at evil.

Christians must strike back and must strike back hard with serious consequences. Resisting evil is not just a game. Resisting evil has epic conesquences. When anti-Christian decisions are made, evil is advancing. Christians must not sit around and let evil advance further and further. Christians must put on the full armor of Christ and take up the spiritual sword ready for battle. It is a spiritual war on behalf of the Kingdom of Christ.

Of course, if they did not keep pushing for anti-Christian actions, active retaliation is not necessary. But if they keep pushing for anti-

Christian actions, then the retaliation has to be quick and powerful. How can Christians resist evil? There are several effective ways to retaliate with desired result of resisting anti-Christian advance.

First of all, an effective tool for resistance can be focused attacks on leaders who pass anti-Christian legislation. It is possible to be very creative in this regard. Letter writing directly to the legislator will be effective. But it's also possible to write letters to the legislator's staff and advisors. It is effective to show support for pro-Christian legislation. If the voices are not heard, then the legislator's camp will assume that it is okay to be anti-Christian.

But it is possible to get more creative than just writing letters to anti-Christian legislators. It is not a bad idea to form a picketing line outside the official office of the legislator who passed anti-Christian legislation. The legislator and his staff will see the public demonstrations and be reminded that there are some very angry people at the wrong decision that he made. It is important to show a personal protest to the legislator who passed anti-Christian laws that will affect all Christians. It will have the possible affect of forcing him twice before making anti-Christian actions again.

Protest does not only have to be directed at the legislator and his office. It is not a bad idea to explore more visible and public ways to attack the legislator who supports anti-Christian legislation. One of the very effective ways to attack him is to attack him through newspapers. The more people write to letters to the editor criticizing or nastily attacking the anti-Christian legislator the better. More and more people will be able to read it. Given that over 80 per cent of Americans are Christians, you will find more people who support your attack of anti-Christian legislator than not.

But why stop at writing letters to the editor. Try your hand at writing an article and submitting it for publication in your local newspaper. Remember, it is an important conflict. If the legislator is left alone to keep pushing anti-Christian legislation, it will adversely affect the Christians (including you and your family) in the long-run. It's important to resist when you can.

Obviously, if you are a Christian journalist and have more ready access to print in newspapers and magazines then you have a greater responsibility to publish something criticizing the anti-Christian legislator. It is important not to remain silent. Silence is guilt. Silence is wrong doing. Silence is to betray the Kingdom of Christ. And as the citizen of the Kingdom of Christ, you owe allegiance to Christ, the King of kings.

Public shaming of anti-Christian writers is a very important part of curtailing his anti-Christian activities. If he is left to give free reign to his evil, anti-Christian campaign, then he will not stop. He must be stopped by the courage and the will of the citizens of the Kingdom of Christ.

Public protest is only the beginning of resisting evil. It is possible to carry out actions with greater consequences against the anti-Christian legislator. The obvious course of action is to try to get the legislator voted out of office. Of course, public attacks help to divest the anti-Christian legislator of supporters. But it is not a bad idea to employ bully-like tactics against supporters of the anti-Christian legislator. If it is possible to bully his supporters to betray him, then the bullying tactic must be employed. You can portray it as a ridiculous thing to support the legislator. You can make the supporters look stupid for supporting him. The point is to get the anti-Christian legislator voted out of office. It's important to use creative methods to get him voted out of office, so that he will not be able to pass any more anti-Christian legislation.

Some may question this technique. Some may think that it is not fair play to get a legislator voted out of office by bullying him or bullying his supporters. However, when we consider the consequences of having an anti-Christian legislator in a place of power, we are compelled to find ways to resist such an evil. It is important to protect the Kingdom of Christ. It is our obligation as citizens of the Kingdom of Christ.

Jesus clearly supports this methodology. Jesus incessantly bullies the Pharisees and the Jewish teachers of the Law. It is important to emphasize that not only did Jesus argue with them, but He also tried to make them out to be jerks. Jesus calls them, "Hypocrites" and "Snakes." Jesus satirizes Jewish leaders as being not genuine. Jesus said that they were praying just to show off to the people. They were not really for God. Jesus Christ questioned their honesty and intention. Jesus tried to malign their character and portray them as evil and conniving. Jesus was, indeed, engaged in the smear campaign of Jewish religious leaders. Jesus did not let a chance slip when he could try to discredit Jewish religious leaders in the eyes of ordinary people.

Looking at it from the outside, it seems like Jesus is the jerk. Why would Jesus blanketly condemn the Pharisees as hypocrites? Why would Jesus not consider the possibility that they were doing everything to glorify God? It is understandable why if we consider what Jesus wanted to do. Jesus wanted the Jews to accept Him as LORD (Yahweh) and Savior. Rejecting Jesus Christ as God necessarily involved rejecting Judaism. It was an either-or proposition.

In order to compel the listeners to follow Him, Jesus Christ bullied the Pharisees and the Sadducees. Jesus ridiculed the Jewish leaders of the law so that those who follow them would feel ridiculous and embarrassed. In other words, Jesus employed bullying methods so that Jews would follow Him instead of Judaism.

Jesus was focused on the goal of His missions. It was important to encourage people to follow Him and not Judaism. We can see that the intention was good. For, it is in Jesus Christ, there is salvation. Jesus taught that choosing Him meant eternal life. Conversely, choosing Judaism meant death. In the reality that Jesus preached, it was important that people choose life over death. Thus, Jesus' employment of bullying methods to encourage his hearers to choose Jesus Christ and life was a noble action. To bully, in this context, is ethical.

Of course, it is clear that the choice is up to each and every decision maker. You cannot force someone to choose Jesus. Everyone must choose Jesus Christ out of his own free will. That is why creativity in methodology to tip the free-will decision in the direction of Jesus Christ is important. Jesus used bullying techniques without apology. There is no reason why Christians as citizens of the Kingdom of Christ should not follow in the footsteps of Jesus Christ.

Especially when anti-Christian actions are being taken and the Kingdom of Christ put into jeopardy, it becomes critical that Christians use creative methodology to tip things in the favor of the Kingdom of Christ. Bullying techniques can be very effective. If creative bullying techniques can compel anti-Christian legislators to abstain from taking anti-Christian decisions, then such a course must be followed. The end is the most important.

Divesting anti-Christian legislator of his powerbase is crucial. Bullying the anti-Christian legislator publicly and his supporters incessantly are good ways to achieve the goal. You will be heroes for the Kingdom of Christ when you effectively bully with the effect of hindering anti-Christian actions from being passed.

There are other ways to strike back. If a legislator is anti-Christian, then Christians can work actively to divest him of financial support. For instance, if you are the owner of a business who gives financial contribution to political leaders, you can make sure that no financial support goes to him. You can also compel your friends, both Christians and non-Christians, to hold financial support from the anti-Christian legislator. The effort to hinder people from contributing financially to him can take various forms of persuasion – over golf, casually over lunch, and in other contexts. The important thing is to stop funds from flowing to the anti-Christian candidate. The more creative you can be the better. What is important is the end result. Your goal as the citizen of the Kingdom of Christ is to make sure that funds do not get to the anti-Christian legislator from any contribution source.

There are other ways to strike back than hindering campaign contributions from going to anti-Christian legislators. More courageous citizens of the Kingdom of Christ can try to block funds access from other government sources. The anti-Christian legislator depends on federal and state financial resources to push his projects through. If he has taken anti-Christian stance and is pushing anti-Christian decisions, then it is important to hinder his other projects so that he will not be able to use the success of his other projects as a stringboard to pushing more anti-Christian legislations. Thus, if you are working with the federal agency in charge of granting an environmental grant to his state, you can do all you can to block the funds from going to his state under his leadership. His inability to procure federal funds for his environmental projects will be a strike against him and will help to topple him politically. As long as the anti-Christian legislator is toppled, he will not be able to pass anti-Christian legislations.

This type of subversive activity can happen from within his own agency. If you are a citizen of the Kingdom of Christ working under him, at any level, it is possible for you to "accidentally" lose the funding application to federal agencies. In the end, it will be the anti-Christian legislator who will look incompetent. More importantly, getting funds cancelled or delayed that he might be able to use will help the Kingdom of Christ in its war against evil. Everyone, from mailroom clerk to the chief advisor, can play an important role in advancing the Kingdom of Christ and fighting forces that seek to destroy it.

The citizens of the Kingdom of Christ have to get more and more creative in attacking the enemies of Christ who want to push anti-Christian legislation. A question arises if Christians are allowed to employ espionage technique in attacking anti-Christian legislators. For instance, do

Christians have the right to hire a private investigator to dig dirt on the anti-Christian legislator? Is invasion of privacy justified in order to defend the Kingdom of Christ? In the past, Christian communities have been cautious about employing espionage techniques to combat anti-Christian candidates. On the contrary, anti-Christian individuals have not been so reluctant to employ private investigators and use other espionage techniques to monitor Christian legislators. More often than not, anti-Christian individuals have used the information derived in such espionage raids against Christian candidates. The most recent was the media portrayal of Larry Flint threatening to investigate Republican politicians.

If Christians are to understand ourselves as being in a spiritual warfare, then should not Christians be willing to employ effective methods to win the conflict? If anti-Christian individuals are employing private detectives to dig dirt on Christian legislators, it follows that wealthy Christians should employ private investigators to dig dirt on anti-Christian legislators. Just as anti-Christians use the information gained to topple the Christian candidate, Christians should be more than willing to use the information gained to topple anti-Christian legislators. In a given spiritual warfare, if anti-Christians are the only ones digging for dirt against Christians, then Christians are bound to lose the conflict.

It is, therefore, safe to argue that wealthy Christians have an obligation to hire private investigators to dig for dirt on anti-Christian candidates. Wealthy Christians who do not use any of their money to hire private investigators against anti-Christian legislators are not doing their part in the spiritual struggle. Wealthy Christians are, in effect, not being thankful. Wealthy Christians are not showing gratitude to God for the wealth that God has given them. Wealth is a gift of God, and wealth should be used to the glory of God. Wealthy Christians have a responsibility. One of them is to hire private investigators to dig for dirt on anti-Christian legislators. Wealthy Christians can afford to do this, and they should play their part in the epic struggle on behalf of the Kingdom of Christ. In this case, hiring private investigators is honoring Jesus Christ, the King of kings and the LORD of lords. The spiritual warfare must be won.

There are other ways Christians can engage in espionage activity against anti-Christian legislators. In the computer age, it could be a good idea to use technology and the internet. Basic searches on major search engines will reveal quite a lot about the political leaders. Furthermore, those who are more adept in computers can hack into the networks of anti-Christian politicians. Of course, the better the hacking ability, more sensitive information can be gathered. There are very good hackers in the world that are Christians. Many Christian teenagers can actually be helpful in this regard.

Hackers can dig into anti-Christian legislators' networks and publish sensitive, embarrassing information on the web. They could do so anonymously and make the web address available via discussion boards and text messaging. More harmful the sensitive date to the anti-Christian candidate, the better. Every Christian, including teenagers, must contribute to the epic spiritual battle that is being fought on the political level. No Christian must consider herself too young to use her computer skills against enemies of Jesus Christ. The battle for the Kingdom of Christ can be won when all play a role.

Hacking into the network is one way to gather sensitive data from anti-Christian candidates. It's also possible to find a way to hack into other systems – such as FBI files and CIA records – that contain information about anti-Christian candidates. This is highly recommended for those who are experts at hacking as it is possible to be arrested for this activity. But if you are arrested in the process of trying to block an anti-Christian legislator from passing actions against Christians, you should wear your prison outfit with pride. You have served the Kingdom of Christ and you have been loyal to Jesus Christ, the King of kings and the LORD of lords. No struggle can be won without all out commitment of the representatives. All Christians as citizens of the Kingdom of Christ must make an all-out commitment. And this commitment must be testified through actual activity. Spying on the anti-Christian legislator with the intent of toppling him is one such evidence of Christian commitment.

Loyalty to the Kingdom of Christ in the political realm is an active process. Just voting for Christian candidate is not enough. It is important to remember that Jesus Christ died for your sins. Without Jesus' sacrificial death you will be going to the eternal holocaust in Hell. It is only because Jesus left His comfort zone of Heaven and took on human flesh in order to die that you have life and meaning.

It is important for you to show loyalty to Jesus Christ, the King of kings and the LORD of lords. It is only right to show gratitude to Jesus Christ. Showing thanksgiving to Jesus Christ involves being loyal to the Kingdom of Christ. Honoring Jesus Christ necessarily involves defending the Kingdom of Christ from its enemies.

It is important for Christians to take this responsibility in the political realm seriously. Christians must put on the full armor of Christ and take up the spiritual sword. Christians must defend against aggressive attacks against the Kingdom of Christ and neutralize threats against the Body of Christ. Christians should willingly use the spiritual sword of Jesus Christ to "kill" the enemies of Christ.

In the spiritual warfare, one way to "kill" anti-Christian legislators is to destroy their viability in the political realm. Christians must make it impossible for anti-Christian legislators to pass any anti-Christian decisions. When they do, they must be attacked publicly and utterly humiliated. Anti-Christian effectiveness in the realm must be curtailed. Any espionage techniques that can be used effectively must be utilized. All Christians must participate and do what they can individually. There is a spiritual warfare. That is why anti-Christian decisions are being made. The Forces of Satan is at work. Christians must resist evil with all that they have.

To say that Christians must bear responsibility in the political realms as citizens of the Kingdom of Christ is like saying humans should breathe. There is a reason why Jesus talked about the Kingdom of Christ. Jesus wanted Christians to see ourselves as members of the Heavenly Kingdom. Jesus wanted us to be loyal to the Kingdom of Christ over all earthly kingdoms. It is Jesus who warned us against enemies. It is Jesus who warned us against spies who attack. Christians are obligated to fight for righteousness and against evil ones in this epic conflict. Christians must do our duty as Christians who glorify the LORD Jesus, the King of kings. It is important for us Christians to treat our political obligations seriously. Christians must be loyal citizens of the Kingdom of Christ on earth.

Chapter 4:

Christian Loyalty and Social Obligation

It is clear that Christian loyalty demands political obligation. In the same way, being loyal to the Kingdom of Christ requires social responsibility. There are active obligations in the social sphere for the citizens of the Kingdom of Christ. And just like political responsibilities, social obligations require execution. It is the sign of active loyalty to Jesus Christ, the King of kings, to carry out proactive actions in the social realm.

Of course, there is bound to be crossover and links between social and political obligations. Often, in order to assert one's loyalty for Christ in the political scene, steps taken will be more properly linked to the social realm. Although there is a symbiotic relationship between the social realm and the political realm, I would like to spend some time focusing on what I would identify as more social in nature vis-à-vis Christian obligation.

First and foremost, Christians must give a privileged place to the Christian Church. Let me explain what I mean. Christian Church is used as a term to refer to all Christian churches which profess Jesus Christ as God. As such, the Christian Church is used to refer to the body politic of all Christian churches. In other words, the Christian Church refers to the ecumenical reality of all local churches in a given nation. It is a representative, visible reality that can be identified by the non-Christian population.

I realize that in positing the reality of the Christian Church, I necessarily distinguish and delineate elements which are not Christian. Thus, to an extent, on a discourse level, a type of us-versus-them is posited. This is not necessarily a bad thing. Particularly for our purpose of identifying the Kingdom of Christ as a separate reality, it is important to identify elements that can be seen as distinctive from the Kingdom of Christ.

In essence, therefore, the Christian Church is being functionally used as the earthly manifestation of the Kingdom of Christ. Certainly, the Christian Church is not the Kingdom of Christ. The Kingdom of Christ is a Heavenly reality that awaits full realization at the Second Coming of Jesus Christ. However, on earth the Christian Church provides the best corporate manifestation of the Kingdom of Christ. St. Augustine described the tension in terms of the Visible Church and the Invisible Church.

Since we live on earth and await the realization of the Kingdom of Christ, it is probably most useful to talk about the Christian Church as representation of the Kingdom of Christ on earth. In principle, the Christian Church is seen as the Body of Christ. Christ is the Head of the Body of Christ, which is the Christian Church. In other words, Jesus is the King of kings of the Christian Church. It is this Christian Church, made up in membership of all confessing Christians, which should be treated in a serious light.

It is important that the Christian Church be given a place of prominence and importance in society. Why? First of all, the fact that we give the Christian Church a place of prominence brings honor to Christ. As the Christian Church recognizes Christ as the Head of the Church, honoring the Christian Church in the social realm is, in effect, honoring Jesus Christ.

Secondly, giving the Christian Church a place of prominence in society provides opportunities for the Christian Church to assert its positive influence in society. If the Christian Church is belittled in the social realm, the Christian Church will be impotent to assert positive influence and benefit the society. However, if the Christian Church is given a place of prominence and power in society, the Christian Church can play an important role in asserting morality and righteousness in society.

Of course, in this regard, it is important to emphasize that the Christian Church is positive and can provide moral leadership. We have to point to one period of modern times to show the tragedy of downgrading the Christian Church. At no time in the History of Christianity, did the Christian Church carry out official persecution of the Jews. Christians fundamentally believe in the right to choose Christ to be one's personal Savior. Because human free will is such an important part of Christian theology. Christian theologians tended to support the freedom to accept Jesus Christ as LORD God. Christian theologians often focused on ways to convert non-Christians to Christianity through persuasion.

But in the age of Enlightenment, the Christian Church in Germany lost its place of power in the German society. It was the age of reason. The Christian Church was perceived as representing the old age. The new age elevated reason to the status of God. Increasingly, the Christian Church in

Germany lost its place in society. By the time of Hitler, the Christian Church was completely impotent to exert any influence in matters of social policy. The weakness of the Christian Church proved a tragedy for the Jews.

Six million Jews were killed by Hitler and the Christian Church was powerless to resist in any way. If the Christian Church in Germany had a place of power then it would have done something. A similar situation currently exists in the United Kingdom. The Christian Church has become completely powerless in the British society. The wishes of the Christian church are of no consequence to the British society. Should there be any kind of social evil, the British Christian Church will be completely powerless to resist. Future consequences of the weakness of the Christian Church is still to be seen.

The case of the holocaust is one example of how a weakened Christian Church would be powerless to resist evil. But there are more important factors than exerting a moral voice. The reason why the Christian Church should be given place of prominence and power is so that it can assert Christian influence in society. Even if the Christian voice may be contradictory to the societal "moral standard," it is important to assert the Christian voice. It is an element of the mission of the Christian Church. It is the responsibility of the Kingdom of Christ.

Indeed, privileging the Christian Church in society necessarily means advancing the interests of the Kingdom of Christ. The mission of the Christian Church is not to uphold some secular ethics. Morality as defined by the larger secular world is irrelevant to the Kingdom of Christ. It is important to recognize that God commanded annihilation in war. Bible emphasized that Israelites kill women, children, and elderly who were not fighting in war. Killing civilians is not acceptable by secular ethics, but it is commanded in the Old Testament. This highlights the fact that the ethics of the world is different from the ethics of God. There will be times that the ethics of the Kingdom of Christ will come directly in conflict with the secular ethics of the country Christians live in.

The obligations of the Christian Church, once it has a privileged place in society through the efforts of the citizens of the Kingdom of Christ, is to uphold ethics of the Kingdom of Christ. The primary ethics of the Kingdom of Christ is to uphold the rule of Christ, the King of kings and the LORD of lords. In order to uphold the honor of Christ, the church must engage in defending Christ from attacks in society.

Thus, when enemies of Christ attack the Christian Church in society, the Christian Church must use its influence to resist. The Christian Church as an important social reality, for instance, can attack Jewish groups that accuse the Christian Church of evil. For example, if the Jews accuse the Christian Church of being evil for attacking Jews, the Christian Church has to retaliate and point out the evil that Jews do. To apologize to the Jews is tantamount to reducing the social standing of the Christian Church.

Jews have done a lot of evil in the world. The most visible example is what Jews have done to the Palestinians. Jews have persecuted Palestinians. Jews have deprived Palestinians of their human dignity. Jews have killed Palestinians indiscriminately at will. But Jews in Israel are not the only Jews guilty.

Jews in England have persistently participated in the evil support of colonialist oppression in Israel. Thus, if English Jews attack the Christian Church, the response of the Christian Church must be to point out the wrongs of English synagogues in supporting the evil program of oppression in the State of Israel. The Christian Church must defend the integrity of the Kingdom of Christ by pointing out that Jews in England have publicly and brazenly supported the State of Israel and refused to respect the ethical realization of the Palestinian State. The United Nations have asserted that it is ethical for Palestinians to have their own state. The United States is dedicated to the peace process and demands that Israel work toward the founding of the Palestinian State. This is understood in America as the ethical thing to do.

In a sense, Jews in England operate from the moral low ground. Nothing Jews in England say regarding social ethics has real merit as they consistently support the State of Israel. The Christian Church has the moral high ground in the global scene. However, the Christian Church in England, particularly, has failed to assert its moral high ground. As it apologizes to Jews without emphasizing Jewish violation of human rights, the Christian Church loses its social standing more and more. We can argue that the Christian clergy have failed to defend the integrity of the Christian Church. But not only Christian clergy should be blamed. All those who are members of the Kingdom of Christ are required to defend the integrity of the Kingdom of Christ. On earth, this necessitates honoring the Christian Church.

What can the Christian Church do? In the English context, the Christian Church would do well to follow the example of the Vatican. The Vatican has consistently emphasized that the Palestinians should have their state. The Vatican has emphasized that the State of Israel was violating human rights. The Vatican has been consistent in their condemnation of the evil that the State of Israel does. In contrast, the Christian Church in Great Britain has failed to assert its moral authority in the situation of Israel. And this failure has cost the Christian Church its standing in society, particularly vis-à-vis the Jews.

There are several reasons why this may be the case. Many Jews have a privileged position in the English society. Often, they retaliate against individual Christian leaders who criticize Israel. English Protestants have, by in large, embraced the Jews, whereas they have not historically done so with the Catholics. Once the Jews were given the privileged status, they used their privileged status to attack the Christian Church. As early as 1800, Jews were found in the English nobility and at the highest levels of the English society. In a sense, English Jews in high positions have functioned to muzzle the Christian Church in Great Britain.

Given this reality, privileging the Christian Church necessarily involves downgrading the social status of Jewish nobility. If the Jewish nobles cannot refrain from attacking the Christian Church, they must be attacked personally. Jewish nobles must be stripped of any functionalist power that allows them to weaken the Christian Church. In a sense, weakening the Jewish nobles and other Jews of influence in England becomes a priority for the citizens of the Kingdom of Christ, who honor Jesus Christ, the King of kings.

How can the citizens of the Kingdom of Christ go about weakening the social standing of the Jews? First of all, every citizen of the Kingdom of Christ must emphasize human rights violations of the Jewish State of Israel. Christians can get creative. The most visible way to do this is to make T-shirts that read, "Stop Israel from Human Rights Violations." Shirts with similar messages can be just as effective. As many English Jews support the Jewish State of Israel, attack of Israel will highlight Jewish immorality in England. As English Jews' ethical stance is questioned, they will be hindered from criticizing the Christian Church.

The more working class Christians in Great Britain gets involved in shaming upper class English Jews, the better. If everyone sees five construction workers with T-shirts criticizing the State of Israel's human rights violations, the message will be more effective than if some upper middle class people wore such shirts. In a sense, the working class actually has greater power to shame English Jewish elites. Working class Christians are obligated to shame the English Jewish elite. To make English Jewish elites ineffective in criticizing the Christian Church is a way to show honor to Christ. Working class can play a critical role in downgrading the status of English Jewish elites.

In America, working class Christians have done their part in making elite Jews ineffective. The fact that working class Christians in America often wear T-shirts with New Testament messages or words like "Jesus is God" necessarily works to silence the Jews. British working class has not been as effective. A part of the reason may be that British working class Christians have been influenced by anti-Christian propaganda of English elite Jews. It is time that the working class in Great Britain show that they are not pushovers before English Jewish elites.

There are other ways to downgrade the status of English Jewish elites. English Christian nobles and Christians of high standing can do their part. And they must do their part. It is important that Christian nobility and Christian working class are united in this regard. Downgrading the status of English Jewish elites benefits both the working class and nobility who are Christians. All Christians have something to gain. Christians of all classes are citizens of the Kingdom of Christ and they owe ultimate allegiance to Jesus Christ, the King of kings.

What can the Christian nobles of Great Britain do? Christians of influence can deny English Jewish elites of privilege. They can pass up English Jewish elites consistently for honors and privileges. In time, English Jewish elites will lose their social privilege. The fact that English elite Jews use their privilege to attack the Christian Church must be seriously taken into consideration.

Besides taking away (or not granting) of privileges and honors from English Jewish elites, English Christians of influence can follow the American example and deny English Jews entrance into important circles. In many places in America, millions of dollars cannot buy entrance and influence in America's elite circles where important Christians are. Whatever the reason, this has worked well to keep wealthy American Jews in check. The fact that British Christians have not been able to do this is a discredit to influential Christians in Great Britain.

Christian Loyalty and Social Obligation

It's about time that British Christians of influence pulled their own weight as Christians. They are not only Christians on Sundays. They are Christians every day of the week. Although being humans, Christians sin every day, it is important to be loyal to Christ, the King of kings and the LORD of lords, in our strongest moment as well as in our weakest moment.

British elite Christians have more to gain than defend the honor of Christ. As English Jewish elites are disenfranchised, British elites will have more honors for themselves. In the survival-of-the-fittest environment, the fact that benefit for the Kingdom of Christ will bring the collateral benefit personally for every non-Jewish British elite should be a motivating factor for British Christians to be creative in disenfranchising and targeting English Jewish elites. There are considerable number of English Jewish elites and their collective disenfranchisement will mean great benefits, financial or otherwise, for British non-Jews. British Jewish elites have chosen to attack the Christian Church. They started the social war. Whatever British Chris-tians of influence do to disenfranchise English elite Jews is a legitimate defense. When the Christian Church is attacked, it must be defended.

Even if some of the elites are not Christians, they can be motivated to attack elite Jews. This will contribute to the defense of the Christian Church. British non-Jews should be reminded of the benefits of disenfranchising Jewish elites. Disenfranchisement of English Jewish elites have long-term benefit for British non-Jewish elites. If a Jew is a business leader, then his lost status will put him in a lower level on the bargaining table. This means that in every business transaction, English Jews will not have the upper hand.

The reason why America has been able to maintain the Christian standing at the top is because America's elite Christians have been effective in disenfranchising American elite Jews. It is commonly understood in America that the most wealthy, most elite American Jews are at the utter mercy of American Christians. American Jewish elites effectively have no power. American Jews have power at the mercy of American Christians. The fact that English Christians have not been able to check the influence of English elite Jews is a discredit to the capability of British Christians of influence. More importantly, it must be seen as a directly contributing cause of the downgrading of the status of the Christian Church in Great Britain.

There are other ways to check the influence of those who attack the Kingdom of Christ. If there are implied physical attacks of Jews who attack the Christian Church, it can be an effective way to hinder the Jews from downgrading the status of the Christian Church. The threat to Jewish safety should be implied rather than stated. But the message should be clear. Given that Jews have suffered pogroms and genocide, implied jeopardization of Jewish safety becomes very effective in checking Jewish power and control in any given society. There is no reason why the Christian majority in Great Britain should become slaves to Jews, either socially or politically. Just like America, English Jews can be made to understand that they exist and thrive at the mercy of Christians, both working class Christians and upper class Christians. In this regard, working class Christians can play an

Christian Loyalty and Social Obligation

effective part in sending a message of threat to English elite Jews.

Some may argue that threat works only when it is backed up by reality. Whether there is real physical threat to Jewish safety or not is actually irrelevant. English Jews already have a latent fear and memory of pogroms against Jews. Even subtle suggestions will increase their fear. Most probably, pogroms against Jews can happen quite easily in Britain (certainly in America), but that is beside the point. The perception of the Jews in Britain (and in the United States) that Jews can be attacked en masse is enough to keep Jews in check. American Christians have effectively used the fear factor to keep Jews in check.

Even the lowest, working class American sees Jews of the highest wealth standing as being inferior by the virtue of being Jews. Many Americans emphasize that Christians go to Heaven and Jews go to Hell. Nowhere in America is Jewish standing secure. No elite Jew can feel secure in his position in America. Elite Jews can be stripped of their social standing or position quite quickly in the USA. Senator Lieberman's standing in the Democratic Party is a very good example of how things can change in one or two years.

Many Jews in America, therefore, talk about "Christian America." They are probably not wrong. Many Jews in America talk about the rise of anti-Semitism in America. They are probably right. The Jewish position in America is insecure and most Jews will confirm this. There is innate disrespect for Jews at all levels of the social class system. Most working class Christians will not want to marry an upper class Jew. Being a Jew has significant connotations and social consequences throughout America. And it is not very positive. The fact that this social perception checks Jewish attack of the Christian Church confirms the current social phenomena as a positive thing. Christians must think in terms of the Kingdom of Christ. If Jews are intent on attacking the Christian Church, they must be deprived of their social standing and power. (Of course, it is understood that Jews who convert to Christianity are Christians. But if they emphasize their Jewishness or assert their Jewish identity over their Christian identity, then it would not be wrong to have them suffer the same social stigmatization that American Jews suffer.)

It is important to emphasize that Christians uphold the integrity of the Christian Church, which represents earthly manifestation of the coming fulfillment of the Kingdom of Christ. Elevating the integrity of the Kingdom of Christ will mean downgrading the integrity of those who seek to attack it. Jews were used as an example of those who attack the Christian Church because they have actually done so. There is ample historical proof and material evidence. It must be remembered that the principle is important. The Christian Church must be honored at all cost. Christian loyalty in the social sphere must be seen in this light.

Although some things are not directly tied to upholding the place of the Christian Church in society, they are integral, in effect, to it. An example of this is marriage. A Christian must marry a Christian. This is a very important point. The Old Testament emphasizes the idea that a believer must marry a believer. There are parts in the Old Testament that command divorcing the unbeliever whom a believer has already married.

Christians marrying Christians is not a choice but an important Christian obligation.

A Christian who marries a non-Christian effectively betrays the Kingdom of Christ. She is being disloyal to the King of kings and the LORD of lords. She is, in effect, committing the greatest act of treason against the Kingdom of Christ. Christians must marry Christians.

In the Old Testament, there is emphasis that marrying unbelievers brought the downfall not only of individuals, but of households, kingdoms, nations, and peoples. The reason why Israel was divided and then sent into exile is blamed largely on the fact that King Solomon married unbelievers. Christians must marry Christians.

The New Testament upholds this principle. A Christian is obligated to marry Christians. A Christian marrying a Christian is described in terms of the relationship of Jesus Christ to the Christian Church. Jesus Christ is the groom and the Christian Church is the bride. The Christian husband should love his Christian wife as Christ loves the Church. The Christian wife should honor the Christian husband as the Church honors Christ. This relationship cannot exist if a Christian marries a non-Christian.

In fact, such a marriage bond is tantamount to an illegitimate marriage in the eyes of the Kingdom of Christ. Despite the strong teaching against divorce, therefore, the New Testament encourages divorce in the case where a Christian is married to a non-Christian. This shows the seriousness of Christian marriage. All teaching discouraging divorce is relegated under the demand not to marry non-Christians.

A Christian marrying a non-Christian represents treason of the highest order in the Kingdom of Christ. A Christian marrying a non-Christian is not only problematic from the vantage point that it is forbidden by the Bible. There are also more practical considerations. If a Christian marries a non-Christian, it would be difficult for the Christian to participate fully in the work of the Kingdom of Christ. It is more possible than not that your spouse can be the stumbling block to your being loyal to Jesus Christ and His Kingdom. It will be difficult emotionally and psychologically to participate in Christian activities which your wife will boycott because she is not a Christian. For the Christian, Christian loyalty must be the most important. No national, racial, cultural, ethnic, social identity must take precedence over the Christian identity as a citizen of the Kingdom of Christ. This identity must prioritize the Christian's life and activity. So, it is far better for a Christian to marry a Christian so that they could work together for the Kingdom of Christ.

In other words, a Christian marrying a Christian facilitates effective Christian work. Working together for the Kingdom of Christ can be a beautiful enterprise. The husband and wife can encourage each other to be loyal. When one spouse is weak, the other can be a source of encouragement. It will be like iron sharpening iron. They can be lovers but also co-workers for the higher goal of Gospel mission. They can work together to be exemplary citizens of the Kingdom of Christ. Practically, a union between a Christian and a Christian can contribute to the advancement of the Kingdom of Christ.

Furthermore, being Christians, the husband and wife will be able to understand the other's loyalty to the Kingdom of Christ. Difficulties experienced from being loyal to Christ are something that the other will be able to understand more fully. The joy at the advancement of the Kingdom of Christ is also a shared experience.

When we consider the issue of Christian loyalty in the social sphere, Christian marriage must be emphasized. We have to stress that although it is important that every Christian desires to marry a Christian, Christian unions require encouragement from other Christians. In other words, it is a duty of Christians that we encourage Christian marriage unions. We should look out for our Christian friends so that they are not tempted to consider a union with non-Christians. In other words, it is the obligation of Christian friends to hinder a union between a Christian and a non-Christian.

Christians must be creative in the way that we block a union between a Christian and a non-Christian. It is important to emphasize that a non-Christian marriage will contribute to the downgrading of the Kingdom of Christ's effecttiveness in society. The Christian spouse will not have support in her Christian life and will be more hard-pressed to focus on proactive work for the Kingdom of Christ. In a sense, hindering a marriage between a Christian and a non-Christian is doing service for the Kingdom of Christ.

Conversely, encouraging a union between Christians is important. It is a way to serve the Kingdom of Christ. Whenever the opportunity presents itself, Christians must help smooth process toward a Christian union. Furthermore, Christians should work together to bring good Christians together.

There should be more active participation in this regard. There are a few ways to approach this. Christians can take a more blatant approach. Christians can be upfront and tell a Christian man and a Christian woman that they are being set up on a blind date. They can spend some time together and see if they would like to pursue a relationship with a view toward marriage. This method may be good if the Christian man and the Christian woman do not know each other.

There are other ways to try to set two Christians up. It can be done in a more informal setting of a friendly group dinner or a picnic. If the group approach is used, it is important that those in the group are sensitive to supporting the environment conducive to encouraging a favorable meeting and interaction between the two. Creating of a favorable environment is important. There is a reason why people go to the trouble to have a romantic candle-lit dinner on special occasions. The atmosphere has a bearing on what transpires. Keeping this in mind is important.

Creating a hostile environment – either intentionally or by accident – may make for an interesting story, but more often than not, it will hinder the object of bringing two Christians together. It is difficult enough bringing two shy people together who are beginning to know each other. There is no use for adding a monkey ranch to make things more difficult.

Indeed, formation of a Christian family must be given priority. A lot of good can come out of forming a Christian family by the marriage union of two Christians. In a way, the Christian family can be the most important social unit (outside the Christian Church) for producing future Christian leaders. Any organization or group will not be able to sustain itself (in purely social terms) if it cannot produce leaders to guide the group through changes and difficulties. Although it is possible to have recent Christian converts playing a pivotal role (as was the case with St. Paul), more often than not, effective leadership requires training. Of course, the training is not by the standards of secular ethic, but by the standards of the Kingdom of Christ and its stated purpose of being chiefly loyal to Jesus Christ, the King of kings.

What are the obligations of Christian parents? Christian parents are obligated to raise their children in the Christian Church. This means that Christian parents must encourage and guide active participation in Christian Church life for their children. Why is this important? It is important to create a reference point for children and the Christian Church must be the primary reference point. Adults are already guided by various experiences and are aware of various reference points. Often, adults are capable of choosing which reference point is best suited for their Christian walk.

With children, before being made aware through experience and cognition, they need to be given an anchor as Christians. The obligation of providing a solid pillar to lean on is provided by Christian parents. Thus, throughout their lives, if their children make mistakes, stray from the truth, fall into error, they can instinctively know to lean back on the anchor provided during their formative years. Studies have shown that children who have been encouraged to participate in Christian Church life often come back to Christianity even when they stray from the Christian Church in young adult years. Those who do not have the formative grounding in Christian Church often are less likely to come back to the Christian Church once they strayed away from the Christian Church.

It is important to recognize that human beings, whether Christian or non-Christian, are under general natural laws. Just because a person converts to Christianity, she does not stop feeling sadness or depression. Christians are happy during good times and sad during bad times, just like non-Christians. Yes, Christians are born again, but the full realization of the Kingdom of Christ will only be experienced at the Second Coming of Jesus Christ. Until Jesus comes back again, we live in the body corruptible, susceptible to illness and pain. Only when Jesus Christ returns in full glory will one be given a perfect body to live forever in Heaven with Jesus Christ.

Assuming that we somehow are completely different as the result of being born again in Christ can actually harm the growth of a Christian as a Christian. Christians sin just like non-Christians. Christians will sin until we die. The difference is that Christians are redeemed sinners whereas non-Christians are sinners still in the state of being damned eternally. When we accept Jesus Christ as our personal LORD and Savior God, we are saved by the grace of Jesus' sacrificial death on the cross. We become righteous in God's sight not because of what we have done or could do but because Christ as the King of kings has declared us righteous in His sight. It is a verdict of an all-powerful King. Christ as God can declare anyone righteous on a whim. The method that Jesus has set is to declare righteous those who accept Him personally and individually as their God.

It is important to understand that every sin Christian commits still deserves the punishment of eternal damnation. One white lie is enough to send a person to Hell forever. And every human being has told a white lie at one point or another. That is why the Bible says that there is no one righteous. Not even one. All deserve to die forever in Hell-fire. But the difference between Christians and non-Christians is that Jesus has chosen to absorb the eternal punishment in His Person for those who believe Jesus Christ is God. It is a rule that Jesus as God has set to guide His created order.

Recognizing that Christians are born-again sinners who are still under pain and misery of the sinful world and susceptible to many weaknesses, the Christian parent has an obligation to provide safeguards for her Christian children. The Christian parent must provide a Christian anchor and Christian stability (or stabilizing element) for her children so that they can become stabilized (or stabilize themselves) when they err. If the Christian parent does not provide a safety-element, it will be very difficult for Christian children to recover from their mistakes. They have no anchor to hold the ship in place as waves strike from all sides. Winds blow and the ship will be pushed this way and that. With a solid anchor, the ship may feel some turbulence and may be moved about a bit, but there is definite stability. You know that the ship will not be pushed far into the deep sea, never to be recovered again. Tougher the anchor created by the Christian parent, safer the future of the Christian children.

Thus, the chief obligation of the Christian parent must be seen as providing a Christian anchor for life for her children. Even if her children starves or have nothing to wear, if she provides a Christian anchor for her children, she is the best parent in God's eyes. God's standards are different from human standards. Often, Christian parents are consumed by the material and not the spiritual. And this contributes to the undoing of their children. Jesus has often warned not to store treasures on earth but in Heaven. Do not worry about what you will eat or what you will wear because the Heavenly Father will provide. Do not fear him who can kill the body but fear Him (God) who can kill your soul and throw you in Hell forever. Christian parents must privilege their obligations as Christians raising children as Christians. Even if Christian parents provide all that the world deems great, if the Christian parents do not provide a solid Christian anchor for their children, then they have failed as parents in God's eyes.

Does this mean that Christian parents have failed if their children abandon the Christian faith as adults? Of course not. God has made it the responsibility of every person to accept or reject Christ according to her free will. God does not want forced conversions but genuine conversion from the heart. Thus, the grown children have the right to accept or reject Christ based on what they want for themselves. Of course, if they accept Christ they will live in Heaven forever with Christ, the King of kings, and if they reject Christ, they will perish forever in eternal suffering in the eternal holocaust in Hell. But they have the right to choose eternal life or eternal death out of their free will.

But Christian parents are responsible for providing the Christian anchor until they become independent adults. Generally, in the USA, 18 years old is seen as the age of adulthood. Until the age of adulthood, while the children live under the roof of Christian parents, Christian parents have an obligation to see to their Christian growth.

Just like parents send their children to school and make sure they do the best they can at school, Christian parents must ensure that their children go to church and receive Christian instruction at church. Catholic Christians in America have been particularly exemplary in emphasizing Christian education. Many Catholic Christians in America go to Catholic schools from kindergarten until college and many actually beyond that. On the Protestant Christian side, Baptists have followed the Catholic example in providing Christian education.

There is a reason why America is 80% plus Christians. The fact that Christian parents actually fulfill their obligations as Christian parents in encouraging active church life or even supplementing church life with Christian school education have lasting results for the Kingdom of Christ.

What are the goals that Christian parents should have? Although a person becomes born again by her personal choice and free will, Christian parents must see their children being born again as the ultimate goal. So, Christian parents should frequently ask their children if they have accepted Jesus Christ as their personal Savior God. You can't force them to accept but you can do all you can, as it is humanly possible, to convince them to accept Jesus as God. The New Testament shows that Jesus worked to convince His hearers of the

Loyalty to the Kingdom of Christ

Gospel message, taught in parables and accompanied by miracles. The hearers may not have been convinced at first. Some might have converted after hearing Christ for the first time. Others may have taken 3 years of Jesus' ministry to accept Jesus as God. And there are some who never accepted Jesus Christ as God.

God gives humans free will. Christian parents must do all they can to encourage their children to decide out of their free will to accept Jesus Christ as God. And until they become adults, Christian parents can force their children to go to church. Giving children the free will to accept Jesus Christ as the Savior God is certainly different from allowing children not to go to church. Until the children become adults, Christian parents must force their children to go to school. Just like a parent who does not force her children to go to school is a bad parent, a Christian parent who does not force her children to go to church is a bad parent. It is the obligation of the Christian parent to force her children to go to church. If she does not, not only is she being a bad parent, she is rebelling against the rule of Jesus Christ in her household. She is dishonoring Jesus Christ, the King of kings.

Cornelius forced everyone in his household to be baptized. It is understood that he forced everyone in this household to go to church. Everyone in his house had to observe Christian forms and practices. Cornelius' example sets the standard for how Christian parents should be. Christian parents must force all to go to church. Whether the children accept Jesus Christ as personal Savior God or not is, of course, up to them. And once grown, after leaving their Christian parents' home, they may choose not to observe

Christian forms. That's their right once they are under the guidance of their Christian parents. Not everyone in Cornelius' household probably accepted Jesus Christ as God but they were baptized and forced to keep Christian practices.

America's Catholic Christians have been particularly good examples of this. Sundays, Catholic parents drag their children to church whether they like it or not. It is no surprise that the Catholic Church in America has steadily grown and the young are particularly proving to be effective Christian leaders. Christians in Ireland are similar in this regard and the number of Christians in Ireland is quite high.

England provides the best example with bad Christian parentage. Not only is it rare to see Catholics in England show up for mass, they do not force their children to go to church on Sundays. So the number of Christians is shrinking dramatically. If anyone wants to see what being bad Christian parents is like, they should go to England. Every church is filled with bad Christian parents who do not even have their children baptized. It is no surprise that Christians have no power, respect, or standing in the larger context of England. Not only do English Christians lack spiritual power, they lack organizational skill and strength of Christian character to raise their children in Christ, the King of kings. Christian parents in England allow their children to go Heathen right under their roofs.

Such Christian parents deserve no respect from Christians just like parents who allow their children not to go to school do not deserve respect. It doesn't matter what they provide in terms of material, earthly goods; they are bad parents in God's eyes. And what ultimately matters is not

Loyalty to the Kingdom of Christ

what is valued on earth, but what is valued in Heaven.

Raising your child as a Christian means ensuring that your child's friend knows this. Thus, if your child brings a Jewish friend home, you must maintain the Christian practice of praying before the meal. In other words, you must force the Jewish child to pray with you and your children. The Jewish child does not have to accept Jesus Christ as God, but as long as he is in your home, he will have to honor Jesus Christ, who is the King of kings in your household. Exempting the Jewish child from your family prayer sets a bad example for your child. It is tantamount to allowing disrespect toward Christ to perpetuate. It is respectable that most churches force Jews to take off their yarmulke when they enter a church in recognition of Jesus Christ as the King of kings. You cannot exempt the Jews in the church. Christ is King of kings of all. If a Jew enters the Christian Church out of his free will, then he must play by the rules. The Jew is not exempt from the Lordship of Christ.

Of course, it is only at the return of Jesus Christ, the King of kings, when the rule of Christ will be completely instituted everywhere. Unbelieving Jews will be sent to the eternal holocaust at Hell and made to recognize the Lordship of Christ from the place of eternal burning. Both those in Heaven and those in Hell will be under the Lordship of Christ.

We are still on earth. It is corrupted by sin, and Christ has allowed Satan to maintain dominion of earth until His Second Coming. But even on the corrupt earth, if a Jew enters the Christian Church, which is to be a picture of the coming Kingdom of Christ fully-realized, Christians must force Jews to submit to the rule of Christ as long as they voluntarily enter the Christian Church. He can choose eternal life or eternal death, but he will still honor the Lordship of Christ. Christ is the Lord of all – both the Saved and the Damned.

America's Christians are generally persistent that Jews who enter their home respect Christian practices. But it is not just in America. African and Asian Christians will not allow Jews to disrespect Jesus Christ if they choose to enter their Christian household out of their free will. Christians have an obligation to honor Jesus Christ as King of kings and the LORD of lords. Christians must be loyal, first and foremost, to the Kingdom of Christ. All human sensibilities and earthly loyalties must be subjugated under the Christian loyalty to the Kingdom of Christ.

Praying before the meal when a Jew is at your house is a good Christian witness as well. Perhaps, it will make the Jewish child curious about Christianity and help him explore more about Christianity. If the Jewish child ends up accepting Jesus Christ as the LORD and Savior God, then you have done something for him that is the best anybody could do for any human being. Now, he can enjoy eternal life in Heaven. He no longer has to go to eternal holocaust in Hell. Saving the Jew from eternal holocaust is a good thing. Not praying is keeping silent. To keep silent and to let the Jew to go to the eternal holocaust without a chance to be saved would be an unkind thing to do. You may be the only Christian in the Jewish child's life who may introduce him to the possibility of life eternal.

Another responsibility of the Christian parents is to do all they can to ensure that their children form good Christian families themselves.

Of course, the first step to ensuring that your child forms a good Christian family is to make sure that she marries a Christian who is serious about his loyalty to the Kingdom of Christ. But there has to be active parental instruction about the Christian family.

A Christian mother can instruct her daughters in the ways of the Christian motherhood. Perhaps, they can read Christian books on the topic together and have a mother-daughter discussion. It will be a good opportunity for the Christian mother and the Christian daughter to bond. So, there will be two positive things accomplished. And the Christian father can talk to his Christian son about Christian responsibilities of the Christian father. It is important to recognize that Christian responsibilities of a Christian father are not the same as the responsibility of being a good father. There may be some overlaps, but it is possible that being a good Christian father may necessitate being a bad father in secular ethics.

A good example of how being a good Christian father can be seen as being a bad father can be found in the area of career choice. If a Christian son wants to enter full-time ministry but he is adequately trained to be a CEO of a big corporation, then the worldly standards dictate that a good father would encourage his material success. However, Christians are under the rule of Christ, the King of kings. The pecking order is completely different in the Kingdom of Christ as it is on earth. And what is deemed successful on earth is not necessarily deemed successful in Heaven. Heaven is concerned with the spiritual and not the material. Earthly things are ephemeral and heavenly things are eternal. Jews in Germany realized how quickly they can lose all their wealth, earthly happiness, positions of privilege, and their life. In a sense, the holocaust is a good edifying lesson for everyone about the insecurity of earthly goods and position. French Revolution is another good example.

  Christian parents must seek to instruct their children about the ideals of being a Christian father or a Christian mother. It does not matter if they as parents often fall short of the ideals. What is important is that their children know what the ideals are and that they strive for it. Being a Christian is more about striving toward Christian ideals. We have to remember that Christians are redeemed sinners. We are redeemed sinners, but we are sinners nonetheless. We will sin until we die. But once we are born again in Christ, we become children of God and live in the grace of the LORD Jesus Christ.

  Christianity, we have to recognize, emphasizes objective truth. Truth is not validated by actions. Truth exists independent of all that Christians do. Thus, even if Christians consistently sin and fall short (which we will), it doesn't mean that the claims of the Bible are untrue. The Bible is true because the Bible is the Word of God. The Bible is true because the Bible is the Word of God. The Bible is true because the Bible is the Word of God. The Bible is true because the Bible is the Word of God. The Bible is an objective truth. Even if 100% of the people in the world denied that the Bible is true, it is true. We can understand the concept of objective truth if we see the example of the earth. The earth is round. It is truth that the earth is round. The earth is not round because we say that the earth is round. Even if everyone said that the earth was square, it won't be square. The fact is that the earth is round. It is an objective fact. In the same way the truth of Christianity is an objective truth. It doesn't matter if everyone denied it. It still will be true.

It is important to emphasize, therefore, the truth regarding what being good Christian father and mother is like. Often, we will fall short of the objective standard. But it is utter mistake to not emphasize the objective high standard (to strive for) because we fall short ourselves. We must not fashion Christianity according to our experiences. There is the objective truth of Christianity which we must uphold. This applies to the realm of Christian parentage.

But the Christian responsibility is not limited to the family. There are other social responsibilities for the citizens of the Kingdom of Christ. Christians have an obligation to become friends with good Christians. It is important for Christians to have good Christian friends and encourage other Christians to have good Christian friends.

The rationale is simple enough. Having a good Christian friend is like iron sharpening iron. Christian friends will encourage us in our Christian walk. Christian friends can help us to strive to be better Christians and hinder us from faltering in our Christian walk. Christian friends can be a type of checks-and-balances. Born again Christians have been born again in the Holy Spirit. The LORD Jesus has bought their eternal life with His precious blood. Christians belong to Christ, the King of kings and the LORD of lords. Christians are a part of a new reality – a heavenly reality. Christians can claim to be members of the family of Christ and citizens of the Kingdom of Christ. As redeemed sinners, Christians will commit sins and may sometimes be indistinguishable from non-Christians, but the reality is that Christians are Christians. There is a fundamental metaphysical and existential difference. Thus, Christians share an identity and a bond that is transcendent of this world. On the metaphysical and existential level, Christian friendships have a big impact. There are real consequences rising from the ultimate reality. Christian friends can reinforce the Christian identity actively and subconsciously.

Having good Christian friends reinforces and encourages our walk as Christians. They will help us to grow as Christians. Christians can help our Christian development even as we struggle and experience difficulties. And Christian friends can help us celebrate as we accomplish Christian milestones. For example, non-Christians will have difficulty celebrating and experiencing joy when a new Christian convert is being baptized. Conversely, Christians will genuinely celebrate your baptism, which is a milestone in your walk as a baby Christian.

Not only are joys felt and experienced empathetically, Christians are bound to be more sympathetic to your struggles as Christians and the hardships you experience. Non-Christians will not be able to understand what is most precious to you – your identity as a Christian. Christian friends can be sympathetic and encourage you genuinely as you struggle in your Christian walk. And Christians will struggle until the Second Coming of Jesus Christ. Support network is very important.

Christian friendship, therefore, are a social obligation of Christians because these networks can be used for the glory of Jesus Christ, the King of kings. Christians can work together for a distinctively Christian work. You can go to church together. You can meet up with your Christian friends and discuss the Bible together. Christians can meet together and pray together. You cannot share this important part with your non-Christian friends. You cannot tell your non-Christian friends to pray with you about pressing issues. Non-Christians do not recognize the reality of prayer and the deity of Christ, who can fulfill your prayers. With Christian friends, you can pray together and your prayer will be answered. The New Testament teaches that where two or more Christians are gathered to pray, Christ will be there.

The promise that Christ will answer prayers is prominent in the Bible. Ask and it shall be given to you. Seek and you shall find. Knock and the door will be opened to you. Jesus promised that whatever is asked in the name of Christ will be given. The promise that Christ will answer the prayers of born-again Christians is a very important hope for Christians. You cannot share this hope with non-Christians. Prayer to Christ can be done only with Christian friends.

There are many other things you can do together for the Kingdom of Christ. You and your Christian friends can participate in Christian missions together. If the Christian Union is holding evangelistic events, you can work together with your Christian friends to getting non-Christians converted.

There are a lot of good things that can result from Christian friendships. Conversely, non-Christian friendships can adversely affect Christians. It is no surprise that it is the non-Christian friend who makes you stumble. The non-Christian friend does

Christian Loyalty and Social Obligation

not care about your loyalty to Jesus Christ. In fact, your non-Christian friend may want to see you violate your loyalty to the Kingdom of Christ. For example, a Jew who does not believe in the work of the Christian Church, may discourage you from being actively involved in the Christian Church.

It is also possible that your non-Christian friend may try to make you stumble by setting you up with a non-Christian boyfriend. It would not be surprising that this can be an important project for your non-Christian friend if she is interested in pulling you away from the Christian faith. Logically, if you can get a Christian girl to go out with a non-Christian boy, the likelihood is that the Christian girl will start losing sight of her loyalty to the Kingdom of Christ. It can be that she is actively working to pull you away from Christ. Given that Christ has given Satan free reign in this world until the Second Coming, it is possible that subconsciously your non-Christian friend is doing the work of Satan in pulling you away from the Kingdom of Christ.

Christians have to actively acknowledge the fact that non-Christians are not loyal to Jesus Christ. This reality has a bearing on friendships, often adversely. Even if your non-Christian friend is not actively trying to tear you away from your loyalty to Jesus Christ, the King of kings and the LORD of lords, it is more than possible that the mere fact that your non-Christian friend is a strong social influence on you can have a bearing on decisions that will impact the Kingdom of Christ.

For example, if your church is having a series of evangelistic meetings and you would like to go and hear the preaching by an effective evangelist, your friend may want to do other things socially. She can pressure you not to go to the evangelistic meeting not because she hates the meetings necessarily but she would want her friend to come along to the event that she would like to attend. There is a type of conflict of (social) interest. This is only one example of how non-Christian friends can affect us in the social scene. But there are many more examples and more serious scenarios.

Having Christian friends is very important. It provides Christians with a support network that can help our loyalty to Jesus Christ, the King of kings and the LORD of lords. Non-Christian friends can hinder our loyalty to the Kingdom of Christ. But our social obligation is certainly not limited to our responsibility to develop Christian family and Christian friendships. There are Christian social obligations that are directed to the society at large.

Christians have an obligation to set up organizations that help the general public and address the needs of the society in which we find ourselves. A good example is providing welfare services. The Catholic Church and the Lutheran Church in America are particularly good about emphasizing social services. Both Christian denominations have organized social work network to help the general public and employ full-time social workers. These social workers are professionally trained and certified by the state to act with consequence in matters of policy and law. But these Christian social workers will have Christian concerns in mind. In fact, this is what distinguishes a Christian social work agency from a non-Christian social work agency. Secular social work agencies are there merely to help people meet material and physical needs. However, Christian social work agencies are there not only to meet worldly and societal needs. Christian social work agencies, by the virtue of being Christian, are concerned about meeting the people's spiritual needs.

In order to meet people's spiritual needs, Christian social work agencies focus on two considerations. First of all, Christian social work agencies are generally concerned about having a distinctively Christian philosophy of social work. In other words, Christian social work agencies often ask how they can make their social work agency Christian in character. The fact that Christian social work agencies ask this question is important. In a sense, the asking distinguishes its character from the very beginning. It is a Christian social work agency and not a secular social work agency.

Some Christian social work agencies try to hand out free Bibles or Christian devotional materials to people they help. Thus, they provide for material needs of patients as well as give them the opportunity at spiritual healing and renewal. The fact that people who suffer don't only suffer physically or materially but also psychologically and mentally shows that a spiritual healing process is helpful. People are complex, and people's spiritual needs must not be ignored. Christian social work agencies often try to meet the spiritual needs along distinctively Christian lines.

Besides asking the question of how to make social work agencies distinctively Christian in character, Christian social work agencies often see themselves in opposition to social work agencies with secular or atheist premise. In a sense, some churches started social work agencies because they felt that secular or atheist social work agencies actually took an anti-Christian approach and even attacked the Christian Church. Some Christians felt that people in difficult situations can be helped without an adverse effect on the Christian Church. Christians who were concerned about defending the integrity of the Kingdom of Christ, therefore, started agencies with a secondary (or even primary) purpose of opposing anti-Christian attacks by some social work agencies. Having a voice in the realm of social services allowed them to be able to defend the Christian Church as an insider. It is important to recognize that sometimes Jewish and Christian social work agencies came into ideological conflict. This is to be expected because Jewish social work agencies prop up Judaism (sometimes against the Christian Church).

  Perhaps the best example of social work agencies in conflict can be seen in the example of Planned Parenthood. Planned Parenthood provides counseling to pregnant women and provide other social services to women. There are good services they provide. However, from the Christian perspective, the fact that they support the use of abortion as birth control is problematic. Because Christians believe that abortion is murder, Christians argue that abortion is not an option. There is no difference between shooting a person in a café and killing your unborn child. They are both unlawful killing and immoral.

  Because many Christians perceived an innate anti-Christian bias of Planned Parenthood, they started Christian social work agencies to help pregnant women. Christian social work agencies of this type actively discouraged abortion. Some Christians provided active arguments from the Bible why the abortion must not be carried out. Other social work agencies added arguments based on other factors. These Christian social work agencies were open to all and actually encouraged non-Christian women to come and receive help. Such Christian social work agencies for women can be found throughout the United States. Great Britain has not been as effective in creating Christian agencies to address important social needs. Unfortunately, even college age and other young British Christians don't seem to see the pressing need of effective and extensive Christian social work network and agencies.

The lack of awareness in the British context can be attributed to the fact that British Christians have been ineffective about creating a Christian culture (or subculture) within Great Britain. Britain is at a stage that most elementary groundwork on creating a Christian counter-culture needs to be done. Further unfortunate is the fact that British Christians will be hard-pressed to find Christian books on the topic in the British context. There is an intellectual and practical gap in British Christianity that requires immediate attention by Christian organizations and churches.

Creating and maintaining Christian social work agencies is certainly an obligation of all Christians loyal to the Kingdom of Christ. Some Christians can (and should) dedicate their whole life to work full-time in such Christian agencies. Manpower is crucial to maintaining and expanding Christian groups and making their social services more effective in society. And all these Christian social work agencies require funds to be maintained and to expand. Thus, it is a Christian social obligation to contribute financially to such causes. Christians, from the working class to the upper class, should find ways to contribute financially to important social work agencies. One can give a pound a month or a thousand pounds per month. The amount is not as important as the effort Christians put into contributing to Christian social work. God sees the heart. Christians can contribute as the Holy Spirit moves.

Besides creating and maintaining Christian social work agencies, Christians can show loyalty to the Kingdom of Christ in the social scene in other ways. Christians can go inside government and secular (independent) social agencies and insert a Christian voice in the workplace and in policy deliberations. Obviously, it is possible to state that Jesus taught such and such in certain circumstances. Christians can be overtly Christian. This can be a good witness because more often than not the Christian voice is inaudible. For many making social polices, the wishes of the Christian Church are inconsequential.

The fact that the Christian Church's position is not even considered dishonors Jesus Christ, the King of kings and the LORD of lords. The ethics of the Kingdom of Christ should be considered. Only people who can force non-Christians and secular agencies to consider the ethics of Christ are Christians. Thus, Christians have an obligation to enter government and secular agencies with the distinctive purpose of making the ethics of the Kingdom of Christ heard.

Of course, Christians can be less obvious about asserting the Christian position. Christians who know the Christian position can push for practices favorable to Christian ethics in a more subversive way. Christians should study the Christian position actively. Once Christians understand what Christian ethics is through active study, Christians can work to assert the Christian position in society. The goal would be for government agencies and secular social institutions to proximate Christian ethics as closely as possible.

Policy decisions favorable to Christianity does not necessitate that all who are making the policy be Christians. What is important is that non-Christians will vote in ways favorable to Christianity. In this regard, the focus should primarily be on decisions of government agencies. There are millions and millions of tax dollars used by various government owned social work agencies. These government agencies affect millions of lives, including Christians. Making government agencies pass policies favorable to Christianity is a way to protect Christians in a nation. More importantly, manipulating government agencies to pass policies favorable to Christianity glorifies Jesus Christ, the King of kings and the LORD of lords.

It is important for Christians to think more seriously about Christian social obligation. Christians live in the society along with non-Christians. It is true that the full realization of the Kingdom of Christ will happen at the Second Coming of Jesus Christ. However, Christians on earth before the Second Coming are to maintain the presence of the Kingdom of Christ on earth. Christians are obligated to expand the influence of the Kingdom of Christ in all aspects of human life as much as we can. These involve impacting political and social institutions. Christians must think in creative ways. More importantly, Christians must act. Christians have to be proactive about expanding the Kingdom of Christ on earth. And this certainly includes the social scene. It is the Christian obligation and duty.

Chapter 5:

Christian Loyalty and Christian Holy War

Christians often have a misunderstanding of Holy War. Some Christians argue that only Islam has Holy War. That is just not true. In fact, Christianity, Islam, and Judaism all have a very developed concept of Holy War. It is, in fact, difficult to spot a very influential Christian theologian, who did not discuss Christian Holy War from some angle. Holy War is an important part of the Christian system. As an idea, the Holy War has received a lot of print space in Christianity over thousands of years. But more importantly, Holy War has been applied in actuality.

Perhaps the most familiar Christian Holy War is the Crusades in the Middle Ages. Some even idealize the Christian Holy War as the most epic Christian war. It is no surprise that many Chris-tian schools use "the Crusader" as their school mascot. Many Christian youths idealize Crusaders. Young adults enjoy reading about the Crusades and various weapons used. Some try to follow war strategies and various battle stories. But for the common public, there are many misunderstandings about the Crusades. The biggest one is that it was a war against Islam.

The Crusades was not a war targeting Islam. Christians were not interested in fighting Islam or perceived it as an archenemy religion. If Christianity has an archenemy religion, it is Judaism. It was the Jewish religious leaders who sought to kill Jesus in the New Testament. The Gospel of John describes Jewish High Priest trying to convince other Jewish priests to kill Jesus for the good of the Jewish people. And the Passion Narratives describe Jewish religious leaders producing false witnesses, buying Judas Iscariot, extorting Roman leaders to have Jesus Christ killed. Historically, Christians have viewed Jews as Christ-killers.

And even after the death of Jesus Christ, Jews continued persecuting Christians. The Book of Acts describes systematic persecution of Christians. Jewish leaders even hired some (including Saul) to persecute Christians. Jews even carried out assassinations and murders of Christians. So, if Christianity has an archenemy in the form of a religion, it's Judaism. There isn't that kind of relationship with Islam.

Even in the Middle Ages, Christians fought primarily with Jews and rarely with Muslims. As Jews lived in Europe, there were more opportunities for direct contact and arguments. Wherever Jews flourished, there are active publications attacking Christianity. In Spain, Germany, Russia, and France, there are active writings directly attacking Christianity.

In the modern-day America, this is also the case. There are many books in print that attack Christianity. A large part of this genre belongs to Jews – both secular and religious. There isn't that kind of hostile relationship between Christianity and Islam. We have to remember that Judaism fundamentally rejects Jesus Christ, and Christianity fundamentally accepts Jesus Christ as God. This is the key defining factor for both religions. This crucial element of definition and identity does not exist in Islam; it is certainly not emphasized as such.

Perhaps, it is Jewish propaganda that causes some Christians to think of the Crusades as a Holy War against Islam. We have to remember that Jews are in conflict with Arabs. It suits Jewish interests to make Christians enemies of Arabs. Jews can play Christians off against Arabs, many of whom are Muslims. Through this way, Jews can use Christians to win the Jewish-Arabic conflict. Someone who may be interested in creating an advantage on behalf of Jews can engage in a type of myth creation to portray a past conflict between Christians and Muslims that was not existent or not that significant. It seems that there may be such factors at play in discussions about the Crusades.

The Crusades was not a Holy War against Islam as such. Rather, the Crusade was a war to conquer Jerusalem and make it Christian. Christians primarily understood the Crusades as a Holy War to conquer Jerusalem for the sake of Christ. The rationale was that it was important that Jerusalem belong to Christians. Jesus Christ died in Jerusalem and was resurrected in Jerusalem. Therefore, Jerusalem was a city holy for Christians. The work of salvation and redemption happened in Jerusalem. It did not matter whom Christians had to fight to occupy Jerusalem and make it a Christian city. The object of the Crusade was to fight whomever that would prevent Christians from honoring Christ's name in the city of Jerusalem.

Thus, the Crusades must be understood as an effort to honor Jesus Christ and celebrate Christ's work of salvation. To put things into perspective, it is important to look at pilgrimages. Christian pilgrims go to Jerusalem from all over the world. The Philippines is over 90% Catholic and there are loads of Philippine Catholics coming to Jerusalem on a holy pilgrimage. In summers, it is not uncommon to see American Baptist church groups coming to remember the pain of Jesus Christ. In the process of the journey of collective memory, Christians are often reminded of the pain that Jews inflicted on Jesus Christ. There is a collective empathy relating to the pain that Jesus Christ experienced from Jewish attacks. Priests and ministers read from the Gospel passages recounting how Jews colluded against Jesus Christ, corrupted the legitimate legal process, tainted evidence, tried to influence the verdict from the inside, and pushed to have Jesus Christ crucified. Via Dolorosa provides a pilgrimage opportunity that reminds Christian pilgrims of the suffering and death Jesus endured to save Christian pilgrims. It is no surprise that emotions run high in Jerusalem among Christians.

The fact that Jerusalem holds value only as a pilgrimage center for Christians is highlighted in the itinerary of Christian pilgrims. Rarely do Christian pilgrims want to visit Jewish areas or Jewish sites. Almost no Christian pilgrims visit Yad Vashem, the chief holocaust memorial in Israel created by the Jewish State. It is probably a good thing because if Christian pilgrims visited a holocaust memorial right after visiting the place where Jesus was crucified, Christians would rejoice at the holocaust death of Jews. Christian pilgrims are in Jerusalem to remember the suffering and death of Christ Jesus, propelled by Jewish leaders and Jewish masses who hated Him. The sentiment would be akin to Jews visiting the gravesite of an "enemy of the Jews" after visiting Auschwitz. They will jump up and down in joy if the Jews saw the tomb, especially if He died a horrible death.

Jerusalem for Christian pilgrims holds value only insofar as it is a place of Christ's death and resurrection. It was that way for medieval Crusaders. Jerusalem was a backward city without any of the modern amenities of England. But Christians felt that they needed to subjugate the city and bring the city under distinctively Christian rule in order to honor Jesus Christ, the King of kings and the LORD of lords. Lords, dukes, princes, and kings wanted to fight in the Christian Holy War in order to make Jerusalem a distinctively Christian city. European people of all classes were willing to abandon their family for the duration of the war and risk dying and never returning to them in order to be faithful to Jesus Christ, the King of kings and the LORD of lords. Making Jerusalem Christian was of the highest priority.

The Crusaders were willing to kill all who stood in the way for the honor of Jesus Christ, the King of kings and the LORD of lords. If Jews stood in the way of Christians occupying Jerusalem, then Jews would be annihilated. If Muslims stood in the way of Christianizing of Jerusalem, then Muslims would be opposed with the full brunt of war. The Christian Holy War was to overtake Jerusalem and subdue it under the rule of Jesus Christ and the Kingdom of Christ.

It is no surprise that the Crusaders were often described in terms of Joshua's Conquest of Canaan in the Old Testament. It makes sense in many ways. The fact is that Jerusalem is in Old Testament Canaan. Christians traveled across vast areas of land to enter the Promised Land just as Joshua did with the Israelites. Joshua faced a hostile people who did not want him to conquer the land. Christians were entering Jerusalem and had to fight much opposition along the way. Joshua was willing to kill everyone in sight who opposed his mission. The Crusaders were copying this philosophy of warfare and were willing to kill everyone in sight who hindered the goal.

In the Old Testament, God commands complete genocide. Joshua and the Israelites were not just ordered to conquer the land, they were ordered by God (according to the Old Testament) to annihilate all living. Joshua and the Israelites were not supposed to kill only the soldiers. God commanded the killing of women, children, infants, and the elderly. God commanded the killing of all human enemies. The Crusaders in principle wanted to obey the command of God in the Old Testament as they modeled the Christian Holy War according to the principles of the Holy War in the Bible. In practice, however, the Crusades lacked the stomach to carry out the genocides. It may not be impossible to find a case of the Crusaders wiping out a Jewish village, which fought the Crusaders and tried to hinder their progress. But in relative terms, they were only a small number.

Some may question the killing of all villagers. But consider this. If civilians are hiding enemy troops, providing food to enemy troops, and helping enemy troops, they gain unfair advantage because of these civilians. Are they innocent? Or are they guilty of complicity in war crimes – of fighting for the enemy? The problem is that the war can be lost if you allow these civilians to continue aiding and abetting the enemy.

A good example of how civilian participation can contribute to loss of war is found in the Vietnam War. Vietnam War is arguably the only war that America lost. The reason that America lost the war in Vietnam is that the enemy was aided and abetted by civilians. Without the civilians, the Vietnam War would have been won by Americans and Democracy instituted in Vietnam. Americans allowed the civilians to aid and abet the enemy and the Vietnam War was horribly lost.

Those who are civilians in appearance can actually function as an auxiliary to the enemy army. For example, if America were at war against Israel, Jews in America may try to subvert American victory from within. Civilians can try to play for the enemy. It is no different in Christian Holy War. The Christian Holy War may (in appearance) be fought between Christians and Jews with distinctive soldier uniforms that distinguish them. However, if there are Jewish civilians in Christian camps, they may be tempted to sabotage Christian victory to give advantage to Jews. Jews can volunteer their services. More problematic is the fact that Jews living among Christians can be tapped by the Jewish side and made (or paid) to spy for them and provide other types of military services. In a Holy War, such civilians batting for the enemy could spell utter defeat for the Christian side. It is safe to assume, therefore, that there is no such thing as a "neutral party."

Perhaps, two Jewish "civilians" out of ten will blow the whistle on Christian operations. However, the two will cost the victory for all Christians. The question is: Is it worthwhile to give the benefit of doubt on account of the innocent eight-out-of-ten and thereby lose the war? In an epic Christian Holy War, it would do well to follow the command of the Old Testament and neutralize all Jews so that the two-out-of-ten will not have the opportunity to affect the loss of the Christian Holy War. Christian Holy War should follow the Biblical laws of Holy War.

The Crusaders did not have the stomach to follow the principles of Holy War as outlined in the Bible. Americans on the other hand did. It is true that American frontier wars were not actually a Christian Holy War. But it is important to note that Americans modeled American frontier wars on the model of the principle of warfare as emphasized in the Old Testament.

American theologians used the language of the Conquest. America's Puritans were God's chosen people and America was God's Promised Land. American Puritans had the God-given responsibility to conquer the land and respect the Bible as the ultimate standard in matters of faith as well as in life (social living as well as individual life). Naturally, American Christians looked to the Old Testament to understand God's principle of warfare. And American Christians waged war and decimated Native Americans. It is the most successful genocidal warfare of modern times. Whole tribes of Native Americans were wiped out, and whole cultures went defunct. And American Christians did not apologize because it was portrayed as a type of Biblical warfare.

It is no surprise that there is a saying in America: "All's fair in love and warfare." Certainly for warfare, Americans have used genocidal warfare as a matter of policy. And genocidal warfare is seen as without limits (or transcending all limits). America in the twentieth century can be understood in light of America's historical experience. America dropped atom bombs on Japan and did not apologize for killing hundreds of thousands of civilians in a minute. In fact, Americans are proud of the action that killed mostly civilians because it won America victory. If America did not kill the civilians, they may not have won the war. In other words, America won World War 2 because America targeted and killed civilians. Americans were ready to commit genocide of their enemies.

America lost the Vietnam War because America did not target and kill civilians. Killing civilians is an important war principle in the Bible. It must be emphasized that God commands proactive killing of civilians. Not to kill civilians in Bible-inspired warfare is to disobey God. Not killing civilians, therefore, represents rebellion against God. The Old Testament is clear on this point. In fact, King Saul is rejected by God and killed by God through human agency because he did not carry out complete genocide as commanded by God. To carry out genocide is being obedient to God's command. The Biblical principle of warfare is clear.

Although the Crusaders did not practice the Biblical principle of warfare, Christian Holy War must uphold the principle as outlined in the Old Testament. Genocide of the enemies of Christ must be a viable option and even a policy in Christian Holy War. The genocide will include soldiers as well as civilians. Children, infants, elderly, and women are not exempt.

In considering Christian Holy War, there are several factors to consider seriously. Perhaps, the most important question is: When is it legitimate to start a Christian Holy War? Christian Holy War is called for when there is a direct attack on the Christian Church with the intent to destroy it. Any movement to destroy Christianity must be treated with extreme prejudice. There can be no excuse for destroying the Christian Church. Whatever "reasonable" arguments advanced are illegitimate by the virtue of the fact that the purpose is to destroy the Christian Church. The excuse may make sense to the enemy side or may even be accepted by third parties. But that's irrelevant. If the goal is to destroy the Christian Church, then a Holy War must be instigated to defend the Christian Church. The Body of Christ must be protected at all cost.

What would be a concrete example of such a case? If the United Kingdom passes laws prohibiting Christians from claiming that Christianity is the only true religion and all other religions are false religions, it is making a move toward destroying Christianity. Christianity is not Christianity without the exclusive claim that salvation is only possible through Jesus Christ. To hinder Christians from making this claim constitutes a trumpet-blowing for war. Passing a law against exclusive claim of Christianity constitutes, in effect, declaration of war against the Kingdom of Christ. It is one thing to say there is a freedom of expression and religion; it is completely a different thing to prohibit Christianity from making an exclusive claim to truth. Without its exclusive claim to truth, Christianity loses its fundamental essence. Christianity hinges on the claim that Jesus Christ is God (the only true God) and salvation is only through faith in Him.

Freedom of expression and freedom of religion will not hinder Christianity from making exclusive claims. But a law prohibiting exclusive claims does. If the United Kingdom passes a law barring Christians from making exclusive claims on behalf of Christianity, that constitutes a declaration of war against Christians in the United Kingdom. In essence, the United Kingdom has thrown the first cannonball calling the Kingdom of Christ into war. British Christians must be spiritually aware enough to see what is going on. More importantly, British Christians must be brave and courageous to resist. Spiritual war has begun.

The question of how serious the Holy War will be depends on several factors. In the context of the example offered, if the United Kingdom actually implements anti-Christian laws in practice, then the Christian Holy War will become more serious. For example, if the United Kingdom actually arrests a Christian making an exclusive claim of Christianity, then it is like a bullet being fired and killing a Christian. Retaliation ceases to be a possibility but becomes a necessity.

The arrest can be under a different premise. When a Christian claims exclusivity for Christianity and says, for example, that all Jews will go to the eternal burning furnace of Hell, the United Kingdom may arrest him for making terrorist threats. But it is clear that the arrest is being made because the Christian made an exclusive claim for Christianity. Christians who are spiritually aware must see through the silkscreen, so to speak. It is safe to assume that a first arrest will be followed by ensuing arrests of more Christians. The first bullet is certainly the most significant and can change history forever.

How can Christians resist the attack on the Kingdom of Christ? There are several strategic ways to proceed. It is possible for Christians to mount a political defense or a legal attack. Ideas relating to this approach were discussed in chapter 3 under the heading of political obligations for the citizens of the Kingdom of Christ. And to a certain extent, discussions regarding social obligations as citizens of the Kingdom of Christ can be relevant to understanding what it means to resist attacks on Christianity.

Perhaps, a lingering question on most Christians' minds concerns the legitimacy of using violent force. In the context of a Christian Holy War, the answer would be "yes." If the United Kingdom sought to destroy the Christian Church and social and political resistance proved ineffective, then militant resistance must be considered as an option. The Old Testament is the best indicator of the responsibility of defending the Kingdom of Christ against the enemies of Christ. The Roman Catholic Church has often applied (rightly) principles in the Old Testament to defend the rights of the Kingdom of Christ. Protestant Christian theologians actually followed the example of Catholic Christian theologians in applying the principle of Old Testament theology vis-à-vis the Christian Church.

What kind of measures can be taken to resist attacks against the Christian Church? There can be planned assassinations of anti-Christian leaders. For example, if Jews in England are motivating legislation against Christianity and motivating arrest of Christian leaders under anti-Christian laws, it is legitimate to plan assassinations of English Jews. As in any warfare, the object is to kill Jewish leaders without getting killed. It is important to do the homework and figure out which Jewish leaders are motivational in propelling anti-Christian laws and policies. Targeting and killing the right Jewish leader is critical if Christian Holy War is to be won. Besides targeting Jewish leaders and assassinating them in the context of a Christian Holy War, it is legitimate to instigate pogroms against Jews who are actively attacking Christians and getting them arrested under anti-Christian policies. If the survival of the Christian Church is at stake, Jewish life has no importance. If killing Jews in large numbers will help to protect the survival of the Christian Church, it is an obligation to kill many Jews to protect the Body of Christ.

Consider this: America attacked Afghanistan in order to protect America from terrorist attacks. America attacked Japan after Pearl Harbor was attacked in order to defend America from attack. America has killed many people, both soldiers and civilians, to protect Americans. To say that America has justifiably engaged in a war to protect America but the Christian Church does not have the right to defend the Christian Church is simply wrong. Just as it is morally justified to kill in order to protect in the American context (or any other similar context where freedom is at stake), the Christian Church (and Christians) have the right to kill in order to protect the Body of Christ. If it is the Jews who are the chief instigators to destroy the Body of Christ, then it is morally right to kill Jews in order to protect the Body of Christ. In other words, if it is necessary to kill Jews in order to protect the Body of Christ, not killing Jews is immoral and represents rebellion against the Kingdom of Christ. Killing Jews is, in fact, glorifying Jesus Christ, the King of kings and the LORD of lords.

How about if Jews are our friends and neighbors? That is actually quite irrelevant. If our Jewish friends and Jewish neighbors are pushing to actually destroy the Body of Christ and get Christians arrested, then Jewish friends and Jewish neighbors should be targeted. It is legitimate to be involved in a plan to kill Jewish neighbors and Jewish friends who have made themselves into enemies of the Body of Christ. When loyalties are in conflict, it is essential that loyalty towards the Kingdom of Christ is privileged. If it comes down to honoring Christ, the King of kings, and honoring Jewish friends and Jewish neighbors, the choice should clearly be for Jesus Christ. To be loyal to Jesus Christ may require killing even the closest Jewish friends and Jewish neighbors. In a sense, killing Jews can become the test of loyalty for the citizens of the Kingdom of Christ. Of course, this would be under the most extreme of circumstances. But Christians must recognize the fact that extreme circumstances can and do happen. Christian Holy War is possible and can certainly become a reality.

If extreme circumstances propel a Christian Holy War, then what are Christian soldiers contracted by a nation to do. In other words, what should Christians in the English army and police force do when there is a Christian Holy War? Certainly, if a soldier or a police woman is a Christian, then she is obligated by the blood of Jesus Christ to be loyal to the Kingdom of Christ and personally to Jesus Christ, the King of kings and the LORD of lords. The soldier's loyalty to the United Kingdom is no longer possible if it violates loyalty to the Kingdom of Christ. It is the Christian duty to resist evil. If the United Kingdom positions itself against the Kingdom of Christ, then resisting evil will mean resisting the United Kingdom. If the UK government orders arrest of Christians under anti-Christian legislation and policy, the Christian soldier (or police) must resist. Refusing to obey orders against the Kingdom of Christ is the moral thing to do as the citizen of the Kingdom of Christ. Obviously, the Christian soldier (or police) refusing to obey anti-Christian orders issued by the UK government will be arrested. But such an arrest is a badge of honor for Christians because it testifies to the loyalty to the Kingdom of Christ. Following anti-Christian orders from the UK government constitutes (for the Christian soldier or police) an act of treason against the Kingdom of Christ. A direct attack of the Body of Christ must be treated with extreme prejudice and with all seriousness required under Christian law.

It is impossible to emphasize that the moment United Kingdom decides to arrest a Christian under the force of anti-Christian laws, the United Kingdom has passed from theoretical opposition to the Kingdom of Christ to an actual (functional) opposition to the Kingdom of Christ. The moment an arrest warrant is issued under anti-Christian laws, the Christian Holy War against the United Kingdom is effectively in force.

All Christian soldiers (and police) who have sworn loyalty to the United Kingdom are released from their oath by the power of Jesus Christ, the King of kings and the LORD of lords. In fact, it becomes Christian obligation to stand against the United Kingdom – more so, if a Christian wears a UK military or police uniform. The test of loyalty becomes crystal clear. There is no confusion. Christian soldiers (and police) must stand with

Christ or with those who try to destroy the Body of Christ.

In the context of Christian Holy War, it is impossible to be loyal both to the Kingdom of Christ and to the United Kingdom. Hopefully, the United Kingdom will not find itself in a receiving end of a Christian Holy War. But Christians in the United Kingdom must be certain that such a scenario can arise and should be psychologically ready for something like that to happen in their lifetime. The fact that the British Labour government is pushing for laws against Christian claims to exclusivity indicates the rising probability of a Christian Holy War on English soil.

There have been cases when the Christian Church clashed with the Secular State. Perhaps, the best known example of the conflict between the Church and the State is the Investiture Contest of eleventh century AD. It is not necessary to go into every detail of the conflict. In fact, it's not really important for our purposes to identify the names of all the players involved. Certainly, there are many books on the Investiture Contest. Anyone interested in finding out more details of the Church-and-State conflict can certainly go to a local library or a bookstore and obtain a book dedicated to the Investiture Contest. What is important for us is to see the principle established in practice at that time.

In the Investiture Contest of the eleventh century AD, the secular ruler and the Christian Church came into conflict. The king (who is equivalent to today's Prime Minister or President) wanted to act in a way that would be harmful to the Christian Church. The Pope in consultation with Christian Church leaders opposed the king. It is important to emphasize that the resistance of the

Catholic Church represents the principle of the right of the Christian Church to resist secular governmental attack of the Christian Church.

It is not a Catholic or Protestant issue. Both Catholics and Protestants are Christians if they have genuine faith that Jesus Christ is God and salvation is only through the saving work of Jesus Christ on the cross. Historically, there were no Protestants in eleventh century AD Europe. All Western European Christians were Catholics. Thus, the action by the Roman Catholic Church represents the common representative historical experience of all Catholics and Protestant Christian denominations. In this regard, the principle indicating the right of the Christian Church to defend the Body of Christ must be understood as a principle for both Catholic and Protestant Christians. The Holy Spirit was at work in the Christian Church in the eleventh century AD.

What happened? In short, the Pope excommunicated the king. You may say, "What does that do?" It did the most horrible thing to the king that he could not have imagined it in a million years. The excommunication by the Pope released every Christian from his loyalty to the king. In fact, the excommunication was akin to the statement that everyone who fights for the king fights against Jesus Christ. It was a clear example when the State chose to stand clearly against the Christian Church. The Pope was full of the Holy Spirit and endowed with the power of the Word of God, so that he was able to resist the secular State and defend the Kingdom of Christ.

In the Investiture Contest, what did it mean for the Pope to (in effect) release all Christians from their loyalty to the king? It is akin to saying that UK soldiers no longer are bound by their oath to obey orders issued by the UK government or UK military command. Thus, if the UK orders a regiment to go and attack, the captain can refuse the order and issue the regiment to attack the United Kingdom, instead.

It is important to see the significance of release of loyalty by the Christian Church. There is a lot written about Jesus' saying that whatever is bound in Heaven will be bound on earth and whatever is released in Heaven will be released on earth. If the Christian Church releases a Christian from his earthly oath and allegiance, that order is binding on earth as it is in Heaven. Obviously, the Christian Church has not practiced release-of-loyalty from the secular State, lightly. The Investiture Contest is one of a few examples where the State came in direct conflict with the Christian Church resulting in the Christian Church releasing all Christians from their allegiance to the State.

What does this mean? It means, in effect, that not only are Christians not obligated by the law of the Kingdom of Christ to be loyal to their secular State, but it further means that any loyalty to the secular State indicates treason against the Kingdom of Christ. In other words, a Christian captain obeying the order of the UK military command represents treason against the Kingdom of Christ, and he will suffer the consequences of his act of rebellion against the Kingdom of Christ when Jesus Christ returns in full glory to establish (in fullness) the Kingdom of Christ.

The Investiture Contest of eleventh century AD clearly showed that this principle worked. Not only did Christian soldiers refused to fight for the king, who was opposed by the Kingdom of Christ, but even nobles and princes refused to give the king any of their support. In fact, Christian nobles and military generals were planning to overthrow the government opposed by the Christian Church.

In the end, the king chose wisely. He repented of his sins against the Body of Christ. The king agreed not to oppose the Christian Church in principle or practice. And the Christian Church reinstated his secular rule. And again, Christians in his nation were bound by oath to be loyal to his government. The Investiture Contest established conclusively the responsibility of the Christian Church to resist the secular State if they oppose the Kingdom of Christ. Furthermore, the Investiture Contest established the obligations of Christians when their country comes into conflict with the Kingdom of Christ. Christians must be loyal, first and foremost, to the Kingdom of Christ and be faithful to Christ Jesus, the King of kings and the LORD of lords.

It must be stated again that only extreme circumstances will initiate Christian Holy War. However, once Christian Holy War is initiated, Christians are obligated to remain faithful to the Kingdom of Christ. This will most likely necessitate opposing the earthly government (actively) that opposes the Kingdom of Christ. It is important for Christians to be psychologically and mentally prepared for possible extreme circumstances.

Conclusion

The twentieth-first century is exciting in many ways. There are unprecedented technological advancements. There is access to all kinds of information through the internet. Education is available everywhere. Knowledge is all around us. It seems like we are enjoying the height of human achievement. And it seems like it is only getting better.

However, despite all the advancements in science, technology, arts, and literature, there still remains the sinfulness of the human condition. Ever since the Fall of Adam and Eve, sin has existed in the world. All that is in the world have been corrupted by sin. Governments and social associations are no exception.

For Christians who are born again through the grace of the blood of Jesus Christ, the King of kings and the LORD of lords, it is particularly important to be conscious of the corrupt state of the world. It is only at the Second Coming of Jesus Christ that the Creation will be restored. Until the Second Coming, Christians will have to live in this world.

Since Satan has been given dominion over the world until the Second Coming of Jesus Christ, it is no surprise that Christians will find ourselves in conflict. More often than not, we Christians will be called into a conflict of loyalties. Our nation may pass legislation directly attacking the Christian Church. Our social associations will try to wrest us away from our obligations as citizens in the Kingdom of Christ. There will be all sorts of pressures to be disloyal to Jesus Christ, the King of kings and the LORD of lords.

It is important for Christians to prepare psychologically, mentally, and spiritually even in times of peace. Who knows when the crisis of loyalty will hit a high pitch? Who knows when we will be faced with the divided road, whereby choosing Christ will mean rejection of our friends and neighbors?

The situation can be so grave that being loyal to the Kingdom of Christ may necessitate standing directly opposed to the Secular State, resulting in imprisonment or worse. Even Jesus Christ, the King of kings and the LORD of lords, warned of such a condition in the Last Days.

We must be ready. We must be awake. We must be prepared. Being ready requires serious thinking about what Christian loyalty means. Not only is it important to think seriously about the implications of being loyal to Jesus Christ in the political and social spheres, it is more important to act.

Christians must stand firm in our loyalty to the Kingdom of Christ. We must be loyal to Jesus Christ even if it means that we will have to suffer on earth for it. We must be faithful to Jesus Christ even if our life is endangered. We have to fight the good fight.

I hope that this book has helped you to think seriously about what it means to be a faithful and loyal citizen of the Kingdom of Christ. I hope that you will think more seriously about it. And I hope that you will use the Bible to think more concretely about what you can do for the Kingdom of Christ in the particular context you find yourself.

How can you be a loyal citizen of the Kingdom of Christ in your city? In your country? How about among your social associations? In the work place? In your family?

May the LORD God Jesus Christ, the King of kings and the LORD of lords, guide you in grace and mercy in your journey as a loyal citizen of the Kingdom of Christ.

About the Author

Sven Pearl Johanson is an American with an Ivy League education who has lived all over the world. Sven has founded Bible study groups in America's major universities and has been very active in evangelizing in Europe.

www.ingramcontent.com/pod-product-compliance
Ingram Content Group UK Ltd.
Pitfield, Milton Keynes, MK11 3LW, UK
UKHW041451180426
11946UKWH00013B/153/J